WM. BRANDT'S SONS & CO.

THE STORY OF A
FAMILY TRADING COMPANY

In Memoriam Peter Augustus Brandt, 1931–2022

WM. BRANDT'S SONS & CO.

THE STORY OF A FAMILY TRADING COMPANY

Edited by Peter Augustus Brandt

Unicorn Press

First published in Great Britain in 2022 by Unicorn Press
60 Bracondale
Norwich
NR1 2BE

tradfordhugh@gmail.com
www.unicornpublishing.org

Illustrations and text copyright © 2022 Peter Augustus Brandt
Photograph of Bill Brandt (page 75) Copyright © *Interiors Magazine*
Photograph of Peter Brandt (page 129) Copyright © *The Times*

All rights reserved. Without limiting the rights under copyright reserved above, no part of this publication may be reproduced, stored or introduced into a retrieval system, or transmitted, in any form or by any means (electronic, mechanical, photocopying, recording or otherwise), without the prior written permission of both the copyright owner and the publisher of this book.

A CIP record of this book can be obtained from the British Library

ISBN 978 1 83839 535 3

Acknowledgements

Special thanks to Abdussabur Kirke for the inspiration behind this book following his translation from the German of Karl Amburger and Henry Bernard Brandt's 1935 *Die Familie Brandt*.

Thanks and gratitude to all members of the family, who have contributed in thought, word and deed to the compilation of everything in this book.

With special thanks to Philip Brandt for his particular enthusiasm and energetic research.

Thanks to Hugh Tempest-Radford and everyone at Unicorn Press for their skill, patience and guidance.

Thanks to Peter for all his personal memories and anecdotes, and for bringing it to us.

Design by newtonworks.uk
Printed in the UK by Swallowtail Print, Norwich

CONTENTS

Introduction	1
Paul Brandt – FIRST GENERATION	2
Augustin Ludwig Brandt – SECOND GENERATION	4
Johann Wilhelm Brandt – THIRD GENERATION	6
Wilhelm Brandt – FOURTH GENERATION	9
Emanuel Heinrich Brandt in London – FOURTH GENERATION	26
Mary Espérance Kalm – FIFTH GENERATION	31
Wilhelm Brandt Jnr. – FIFTH GENERATION	35
Augustus Ferdinand Brandt – SIXTH GENERATION	43
Ludwig Walther Brandt – SEVENTH GENERATION	50
Walter Augustus Brandt – EIGHTH GENERATION	55
Peter Augustus Brandt – NINTH GENERATION	62
Maps	134

INTRODUCTION

In 1937, Dr Erik Amburger, a relative of the Brandt family and a renowned historian, presented a German genealogy of the older Brandts in Hamburg. His book, sturdily bound in linen and scholarly in detail, has been in our family's possession ever since and has attracted to itself numerous additions, inserts and handwritten marginal notes, making it a focal point for the now extensive record of our family line. I have other documents of this history at home; yet more are archived at Nottingham University. The present book uses a translation of Dr Amburger's work as a starting point, then goes on to explore the development of my line of the Brandt family, and my life in particular, as a way to tell the story of the Brandt business activities down into the twentieth century. And it has been business – trading and banking – which has formed a constant thread throughout. The book also includes my personal life story. The Brandt businesses have always been family affairs, tied closely to the lives of those who carried them on.

The origins of our mercantile inclinations cannot be fully traced. Paul Brandt, who is the earliest known ancestor, was active in Stettin sometime before 1686, but every attempt by my research predecessors Dr Pfingsthorn and Dr Amburger to trace him in Stettin failed. A pastor named Peter Brandt was married in Stettin to Maria Schultze on 15 July 1659, and apparently his children were baptised in his parish of Dedelow near Prenzlau in the sparsely populated, lake-strewn region of Uckermark. That Parish's church registers, however, only begin in the year 1678, which means we may never know whether or not Pastor Peter Brandt was Paul's father. This means Paul Brandt is our earliest known forefather, and it is with him that I will begin.

Paul Brandt
FIRST GENERATION

Paul Brandt, my sixth-great-grandfather and the earliest recorded ancestor of the Brandt Line, moved as a merchant from Stettin to Hamburg. Stettin is now just over the German border in Poland where it is known as Szczecin, but historically it had been a German city and a member of the Hanseatic League since 1278.

In 1630, Stettin fell under Swedish rule, which led to severe economic decline and lasted until 1720, when it was absorbed into Prussia. Paul Brandt, therefore, emigrated from the town during a period in which the city was cut off from its former trading partners.

We know that he moved to Hamburg in or before 1686, because on 26 February of that year he is recorded as paying the first half of the fee for *Bürgerrecht*, or the Right of Citizenship. Peculiar to Hamburg and abolished in 1918, *Bürgerrecht* could be acquired for a fee or was inherited by the owners of bequeathable land within the city limits. Its holders enjoyed privileges bestowed on them by the *Stadtherren*, or city lords. Paul Brandt obtained his *Bürgerrecht* after paying the remainder of the fee on 31 December 1690.

We do not know when he died, but in 1687 he married Gerdruth von Essen. This we know from the proclamation of the wedding on 28 August, although that was not necessarily its precise date. The same goes for many of the marriages and births mentioned in this account, which are commonly known by proclamations and records of baptism respectively. Paul's wife Gerdruth, for example, was baptised at St. Jacobi Church in Hamburg on 7 September 1670, so would probably have been born shortly beforehand, as the emphasis in an age of Christian belief and infant mortality was on baptising a child quickly to safeguard the soul of the child – and the parents. Gerdruth was the daughter of the sugar manufacturer Jacob von Essen and his wife Anna Hinrichs. The date of her death, like his, is not recorded.

They had four children together: Jacob, Augustin Ludwig, Anna and Paul. The second of these, Augustin Ludwig, was my fifth-great-grandfather.

Augustin Ludwig Brandt
SECOND GENERATION

Augustin Ludwig Brandt was baptised at the Nikolaikirche in Hamburg on 26 December 1689. He was a merchant like his father and became a Citizen of Hamburg at the age of 31. His standing must have risen further still when he became a *Jurat* at St. Jacobi Church in 1747. This elected position entailed responsibilities for the parish of one of Hamburg's principal churches, namely: overseeing the parish's assets, keeping registers of its properties, collecting income, deciding on expenses and keeping accounts.

Augustin resided at Kleiner Jungfernstieg in the very centre of today's Hamburg. Jungfernstieg became the first German street to be asphalted, but that was much later in 1838. In my fifth-great-grandfather's time, it would have been cobbled. Augustin was the first of our line to bear the Brandt coat of arms.

The Brandt coat of arms, 1747.

He married the twenty-year-old Josephine Cäcilie Tievoigt in 1727, but this union was cut very short by her death soon afterwards.

Almost exactly a year later, on 15 June 1728, Augustin married Susanna Catharina Volckmar at Hamburg's Michaelis Church. She had just turned 23 and was the daughter of Theodor Friedrich Volckmar, Syndic of the Holsteinian Estates, and his wife Ester Jenisch.

Augustin Ludwig Brandt died on 2 August 1758 and was buried at St. George's Church five days afterwards. His wife of thirty years was named as the guardian of their three surviving children. She herself died sometime after 1767.

Augustin and Susanna Catharina are recorded to have had four children together: Johann Wilhelm, Paul Ludwig, Anna Elisabeth and Anna Catharina. The first of these, Johann Wilhelm, was my fourth-great-grandfather.

Johann Wilhelm Brandt
THIRD GENERATION

Johann Wilhelm Brandt was born in Hamburg on 29 December 1736 and baptised at home in the parish of St. Catherine on the first day of the new year. His godparents were Captain Johann Wilhelm Gildenhusen, Christoffer Meyer and Rebecca Brandt.

Nothing is known about Johann Wilhelm's youth or how he started his business. He purchased the right to Hamburg Citizenship in 1760, for which he was sponsored by Emanuel Jenisch, a man who would play a further role in his life and that of his sons.

In 1766, he married 21-year-old Hanna Magdalena Sievers. She had been born in Hamburg to the merchant Johann Georg Sievers and his wife Hanna Burmester. During the first few years of his marriage, he lived on Kleiner Jungfernstieg in the parish of his birth. He was registered as a broker in April 1770; for this he had to pay a one-thaler annual subscription to the *Präses Commercii*, Hamburg's president of Commerce. He dedicated himself to the insurance business. Johann Wilhelm moved house in 1770 and went to live in the parish of St. Michael, then moved again two years later, this time into the house of J. J. Schacht on Schachtstraße, or nearby, in the parish of St. James, for which the rent was 150 thalers. A thaler in Hamburg at that time probably had a silver content of around 25 grams, which would imply a rent equivalent to 121 troy ounces of silver, worth today around £2,200 – although the modern value of silver is volatile.

It was at that house that his daughter Anna Juliane Pauline was born in 1773, and his son Emanuel Heinrich in 1776; they were the first of his children not to die in infancy. Wilhelm and Hanna Magdalena moved to the house of J. C. Amberg's widow near St. Peter's Church in time for Ascension Day, and there his last child Wilhelm was born. Hanna Magdalena died there in 1780 at just 35 years of age.

After three years as a widower, Johann Wilhelm became engaged on 8 April 1783 to Margaretha Johanna Goverts, daughter of the insurance broker Hermann Goverts and his wife Maria Hermans Elking. She was less than a year younger than him. Emanuel Jenisch, a cousin of his mother and also his benefactor, hosted the wedding at his house; a certain Pastor Rüter conducted the ceremony.

The master of the Brandt household fell seriously ill with bilious fever in February 1791, just after his daughter had married Luer Brüst. He recovered only slowly. His youngest son left home in the summer of 1793. With only one child left at home they moved again, on 1 June 1797, into the house of Johann Wilhelm's brother-in-law Hermann Goverts at Herrlichkeit, down towards the port, for which they paid 500 thalers.

That house became the property of J. C. Goetgens the same autumn and the Brandt family moved on or around Ascension Day 1798 into the house of the widow Anna Elisabeth Dendas at 123 Neuer Wall, for which they paid 1200 thalers in rent. Neuer Wall is nowadays a highly prestigious Hamburg shopping street. Such a rapid rise in rental is explained by the currency debasement of those crisis years. They now lived in the parish of St. Nicholas: this means that over the course of thirty years, Johann Wilhelm and his family had belonged to all five of Hamburg's main parishes.

In the final years of his life, Johann Wilhelm had to endure the death of his daughter, and then, after his son Wilhelm had returned from Russia, he bade farewell to both sons as they moved away. He then witnessed the miscarriage of their voyage when their ship was captured. He died on 16 September 1800 after a short illness and was buried three days later in the cemetery at St. Peter's Church. His business was carried on by his brother-in-law Goverts until his son Emanuel Heinrich returned, having hurried back home from England upon news of his death. This son paid for half the rental of the apartment on Neuer Wall and for the maintenance of the little household from December 1800 onwards. Mrs Margaretha Johanna, however, followed her husband within the year at the age of 63 and was buried in the graveyard at Dammtor.

Johann Wilhelm and his first wife had six children: Susanna Pauline, Raetke Joachim, Christoph Eberhard, Anna Juliane Pauline, Emanuel Heinrich, and lastly Wilhelm, my great-great-great-grandfather, by whose illustrious name our family business ultimately became known.

Pages from *Denkmahl der Freundschaft* (Friendship Memorial), Hamburg, 1793. The surnames Beil, Goverts and Philippi appear several times in the 160 indexed pages of hand-written testaments of friendship.

This seal is said to date from *c.*1770, suggesting that it belonged to JW, although it has the initials WB on it. We can only speculate, but perhaps JW was known as W.

Wilhelm Brandt
FOURTH GENERATION

So far I have been able to relate relatively few details of my ancestors, but this is not the case with Wilhelm Brandt, due partly to his nearer proximity in time, partly to the greater extent of his activities and renown.

He was born in Hamburg on the first day of 1778 and baptised on the fourth. His godparents were Anna Maria Grotian, Guilliam Clamer and Friedrich Rohlffs.

Wilhelm lost his mother at the tender age of two and was motherless until his father remarried in 1783 when he was five. His father paid the first schooling subscription for the three-year-old for future lessons with one Mrs Thamsen, and two years later he was entrusted to Marie Volger and the tutor J. A. Schmidt. These lessons ended in 1789, whereupon Wilhelm and his brother began to learn French and English with other tutors. By then it was time to begin a commercial apprenticeship. The boy, who was, according to Dr Amburger's account, intellectually far superior to his older brother Emanuel, was lucky enough to be sent straight abroad, a tradition that would reappear for later Brandts, myself included. He was confirmed on 10th September 1792 while the necessary items were being procured to equip him for his new situation. Faraway Archangel had been chosen, which is explained by the relations they already had living there. Johann Wilhelm Brandt's daughter Juliane had married Luer Brüst in 1791, whose sister Maria Sara had been the first wife of Hermann Friedrich Goverts, Johann Wilhelm's brother-in-law. The other sister, Margarethe Brüst, married the Archangel merchant Alexander Christian Becker and moved to Altona with her family in 1792 where she was able to circulate among her new relatives in Hamburg. Wilhelm was taken on as an apprentice in Becker's business in Archangel. He set sail from Hamburg on 12 June 1793, landing

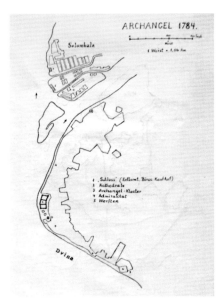

Plan of Archangel, 1784.

safely at his destination after a six-week sea voyage around the top of Norway. He remained in Archangel for five years without interruption, acquiring' a solid commercial training. Many foreign, mostly German, Dutch and English traders and business people lived permanently in Archangel, some of them for generations. The city's entire sea trade was under their control. Numerous people who were only temporarily in Archangel also worked in these people's offices. It was in those circles that Wilhelm moved. He became especially friendly with Jakob Berend Rodde, a cousin of Becker's, who had been born in Stade in Germany, but whose father was from Moscow.

Five years later, Wilhelm left Archangel and returned to Hamburg via Petersburg and Lübeck, arriving in December 1798. He took the Citizen's Oath together with his brother in 1799, whereupon Emanuel Jenisch, that good friend and benefactor, made both brothers 'supercargos' on a vessel bound for the West Indies. The resourceful Wilhelm had determined to seek his fortune across the Atlantic after completing this assignment. His father had been an insurance broker and, given what we now know of Wilhelm, this must have seemed a limited horizon for him. Going to the Americas was not an uncommon choice at that time. The Kleinworts, a German family with a similar background and development, went there and traded in sugar and cigars. The Baring family, German merchants who had become bankers in the previous century, also went to the southern part of the United States.

Wilhelm's older brother Emanuel Heinrich was to act as his escort on the westward voyage, since he was just 21 years old. But these American plans never came to anything. England had been at war with Revolutionary France for years and English privateers lurked in the Channel. Jenisch's ship fell to them, having been destined firstly for Bordeaux, which its papers showed accordingly, allowing the British to claim that they were trading with the enemy. The vessel was brought to the roads off Cowes and its cargo confiscated. The Brandt brothers spent months trying to release the goods. Their negotiations at the Admiralty Courts finally bore fruit in the summer of 1800 – but then news of their father's death arrived. Emanuel hurried home while young Wilhelm stayed behind to oversee the unloading of the ship. Only then could he return to Hamburg. Once the inheritance had been settled, he was in a position to begin his own business; but he did not remain in Germany, nor did he cross the Atlantic but returned to the place of his apprentice years: Archangel.

In 1802 he founded the firm Brandt, Rodde & Co. together with his friend Jakob Berend Rodde. This new trading house, like all foreign firms in Archangel, carried on commission business, importing colonial goods and exporting local Russian produce. Alexander Christian Becker Jr., a son of Wilhelm's former employer, entered the firm as a partner the same year, but parted ways from Brandt and Rodde in 1807. During those five years the company was called Becker, Brandt & Rodde.

In December 1803, the young Wilhelm Brandt married Elisabeth Wendeline van Brienen, herself just 15 years old and a daughter of the head of a company which was not only the oldest in the town but also for decades the leading trading firm at Archangel. Its origins were that

Wilhelm Brandt Snr., 1778–1832.

Roderick van Brienen had been engaged by Peter the Great to build the docks and harbour works at Archangel in 1690, and there his family had remained.

Shortly before Wilhelm's wedding, Rodde had married a daughter of the firm's second owner, Salomon van Brienen. Strong family and commercial ties were thus established at Archangel.

Business flourished rapidly, especially once Wilhelm had persuaded his brother Emanuel to set himself up in London as his agent (more of which later), a move which would prove providential for our branch of the family. In 1806, he and his wife and son moved to Hamburg to manage his affairs from there. The Archangel business remained entrusted to Rodde. Difficulties inflicted on trade by Europe's political situation were happily overcome. The capturing of vessels and the Continental Blockade – measures by which Napoleon hoped to bring England to its knees – made little impact on their healthy affairs. By 1809 they had already overtaken R. van Brienen Söhne & Co. in Archangel and assumed the leading position in trade statistics. Hamburg was seized by

THE STORY OF A FAMILY TRADING COMPANY

Elisabeth Wendeline van Brienen, 1788–1826.

the French in 1810, and Wilhelm moved back to Archangel the following year.

The year previously, he had had a sugar refinery built there and it was to this factory that he turned his special attention. Much later, the same building was to become the principal courthouse for the region. Rodde

Sugar Refinery.

13

left the company in 1812 and in 1813 Wilhelm gave up the commission business and confined himself to the manufacturing of sugar. Only when peace returned to Europe did he resume his former activities. In 1816, he made Johann Georg Classen *Prokurist*, or authorised signatory – an important position in German businesses – of the extended company Wm. Brandt & Co., gave him the leadership in Archangel, travelled to Petersburg with his family in March, and then went on via Lübeck to Hamburg where he took up residence once again. He had a country house built by Axel Bundsen in Othmarschen on the Elbe, below Altona, at what is now number 186 Elbchaussee. Othmarschen has since become an upmarket suburb in the west of Hamburg. Tradition holds that the master builder was asked to model it on a house in the Crimea. It was a two-storey, flat-roofed structure with a protruding semi-circular terrace supported by Doric pillars. The rooms inside were grouped around a domed hall which extended up through both floors. The central room upstairs was decorated with a mural depicting a Crimean landscape. The house was situated within extensive parklands of which only a fraction now remains. The family spent happy years there and the children went to school in Hamburg.

Brandt's Landhaus.

THE STORY OF A FAMILY TRADING COMPANY

Business in Archangel flourished quickly once again. Wm. Brandt & Co. built up its own fleet, most of which, according to Hamburg custom, bore the names of family members. A network of agents spanned western Europe. The family house in Archangel, which was by then occupied by Wilhelm's *Prokurist* Johann Georg Classen, was the finest in the city, and was thus chosen as quarters for Tsar Alexander I when he visited the city

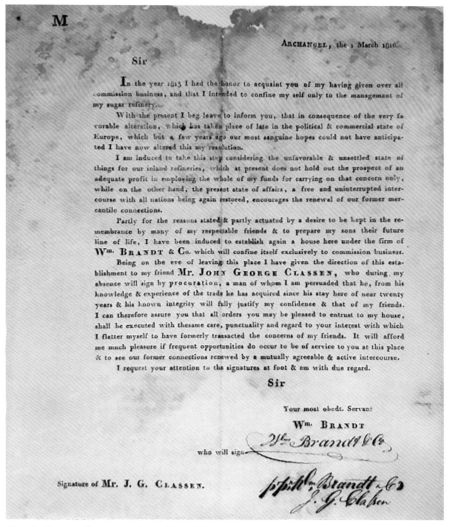

Circular from William Brandt, Archangel, 1816.

in 1819. A very telling account of this visit which has remained in the possession of the Classen family in Hamburg is reproduced here:

> Archangel, 2 August 1819.
>
> My Beloved Brother!
>
> The purpose of me writing to you is to share with you, our aged mother and our siblings the great good fortune that befell us this week. Our magnanimous Emperor, the liberator of Russia and all Europe, He with whom the Hand of Providence clearly resides, and who equally clearly stands out above all monarchs on account of his genuine Christian humility and strong sensibility, favoured our Archangel with his presence for three days, and mine was the honour of accommodating this most gracious of all princes beneath my roof. You will probably have heard from Brandt that my house, which I purchased from him before he left here, had been chosen to accommodate the Emperor, partially on account of its comfortable interior appointments, but principally because of its fine situation and prospect. As you can well imagine, I enjoyed mobilising everything in my power to prepare my household, inside and out, to receive this most precious guest as comfortably and hospitably as possible. I even ordered the finest fruits to be couriered from Petersburg, which alone cost 1,200 roubles and which – alas! – all arrived completely spoiled, with the exception of the pineapples and grapes.
>
> The Monarch arrived on the evening of Monday 28 July, or rather at midnight; I will not attempt to describe the cheering and rejoicing of the people of this city, which has not seen a Russian monarch within its walls since Peter the Great, 117 years ago. I will tell you only that, during the three-day stay of our Emperor, which was favoured by heaven with the finest weather, a cheerful crowd of people circulated before my house from early in the morning until deep into the night, around 2 o'clock, in order to catch sight of him, whom they welcomed, every time he showed himself at the windows or on the balcony, with a thousand unified hurrahs! I will also mention only briefly that the Monarch was

very satisfied with the orderliness of the city and with all of its public buildings and institutions, and stated repeatedly that he found all of them far exceeding his expectations. This placed him in such a cheerful mood that his entourage unanimously confirmed he had never been so jovial and magnanimous for three consecutive days anywhere on his travels in Russia. Not only did he distribute numerous expressions of favour among many individuals, he also conferred substantial easements upon our city and our trade, and promised yet more still. More of that another time – now I will hurry to tell you what affected me personally, that which indeed still seems to me a dream, so completely did the benevolence and humility of our noble Monarch towards us exceed everything that we even dared to expect on account of his known lenience and humanity.

I received the Emperor, who, as I said, arrived at midnight, on the steps, where he greeted me in friendly fashion, asking whether I was the man of the house; he then entered upon the rooms. Our War Governor Admiral Klokachev and the Civil Governor were allowed in for an audience; then, at around 1 o'clock, I was called to the Emperor; I spent almost a quarter of an hour quite alone with him. He spoke French with me, and although it embarrasses me acutely to speak French, his lenience and geniality not only gave me the composure and sobriety I needed to speak with candour and forthrightness, it also made it easier for me to speak French than ever before. Afterwards I immediately wrote down most of our discussion and I will tell you of it when the opportunity arises; every one of his utterances bore, like his mien and countenance, the stamp of his beautiful heart, the imprint of pure humanity. After me my wife was called to him, and she too came out of his room with tears in her eyes, greatly moved; the Monarch had mentioned with much kindness her only brother, the *Polizeimeister*[1] Bröcker in Petersburg, towards whom he is very well disposed, and he was so humble as to kiss her hand

---

1 A police officer. In modern usage this refers to a mere constable, but given that the Emperor knew him, it may have meant something higher than that then. Its literal meaning is 'police master'.

when she departed. You can well imagine, dear Georg, how much we delighted in these tokens of Imperial graciousness, and yet that was not all we were to enjoy.

On the two following days, Tuesday and Wednesday, the Emperor dined at home, and both times I had the good fortune to be summoned to table on his command. Through a misunderstanding I was not told on the first day that I was to enjoy that honour. I was sitting quietly in my *comptoir* when a valet of the Emperor hurried in and told me I should come to table, and then another valet arrived and added that the Emperor did not wish to sit and dine before the man of the house was there – and indeed, two minutes later, after I had thrown on a mere frock-coat, I entered the dining room and found the Emperor standing surrounded by 14 Generals and Excellencies, waiting only for me. I relate to you this minor incident to give you an idea of the extent of the humanity and humility of the foremost Monarch on earth. After dining, his Adjutant General, Prince Volkonsky, who also stayed at my home, a man who possesses and deserves the Emperor's complete trust, said to me that the Monarch wished to see my children and would therefore take tea with us at eight; this is because we were accommodated in cramped and not altogether elegant quarters in the apartment of one of our kitchen staff. The Emperor came quite alone, gave his arm to my wife who awaited him on the steps, took tea with us, conversed with us animatedly about many things, addressed my eldest daughter many times with much kindness, caressed our youngest girl, and was again, in my presence, humble enough to kiss the hand of my wife upon departing. When on the following day, Wednesday, I had the good fortune to be called to dine a second time, we sat only eight of us at a small round table: the Emperor, five of his suite, the War Governor and I; the Emperor was unusually cheerful, joking, laughing and conversing with each and every one at the table in an entirely unforced manner, sometimes in Russian, sometimes in French. Straight after dining the Emperor drove through the Port to the fortress twenty versts away and at ten o'clock honoured with his presence a ball hosted by the merchants of the town, the most resplendent Archangel has ever seen. He remained until twelve o'clock and my wife had twice the good fortune, my daughter once, to be invited by him to dance some rounds of the polonaise.

The following day, Thursday, was the day of the Emperor's departure; numerous of the Emperor's expressions of favour had already been distributed by the War Governor and people had amassed before my house and in the courtyard when I was called by Prince Volkonsky. As I entered the Prince said to me: l'Empereur m'a ordonné de vous témoigner Sa parfaite satisfaction de la réception qu'il a eut dans votre maison et pour signe de sa reconnaissance il vous fait remettre par moi une bague pour vous et des bijoux pour votre épouse et votre fille.[2] With those words he handed me three Morocco leather boxes, one of which contained a precious ring for me, another an *esclavage* for my wife, and a third a *fermoir* for my daughter, all of which were inlaid with diamonds and crafted with the utmost taste. Experts have estimated this truly Imperial gift to be worth 15,000 roubles, but to us these tokens of Imperial benevolence are of inestimable worth and will be, God willing, handed down to our great-grandchildren.

This happened around ten o'clock in the morning; at twelve o'clock the Emperor drove out to the Admiralty where we enjoyed the fine pageant of the launch of two warships, and then he ate with the War Governor, returned home around four o'clock and prepared for his departure. At five o'clock I was called to the Emperor. He thanked me with the utmost humility for the good reception he had enjoyed, apologised for making so much difficulty for us, asked whether I would take him into my house again should he visit Archangel once more, and so on – I could barely reply with anything but tears, so moved was I, since for a man of feeling there is no finer sight than that of cultivated humanity on the throne. As he released me he kissed me five times, and then he had my wife and daughter called in; they too left his room a few

---

2 "The Emperor has ordered me to tell you of his perfect satisfaction at the reception he has been given at your house, and as a sign of his gratitude he gives you a ring for yourself and jewelry for your wife and daughter.

minutes later sobbing loudly. Never will the impression of this scene which my pen fails to describe be erased from my memory. Everyone in the Emperor's suite assured me that on all his travels in Russia he had never been so extraordinarily magnanimous and humble towards his host. I like to flatter myself, therefore, with the thought that we had the good fortune to be personally pleasing to the Monarch, and if that is so then it can only be because of the pure, unvarnished expression of our love, the candour and forthrightness of my utterances, the matronly appearance of my wife and her striving in her every attention to him, and the unaffected naturalness of my daughter. Whatever may happen to us, these three days have been the most extraordinary of my life.

Please relate the content of my letter to our honourable mother, for whom Heaven has reserved such a pleasure until her 86th year, and to our siblings and friends. Should I not have the time to write at such length to Brandt then I shall refer him to you for more details, and I am sure he will delight wholeheartedly in the good fortune that has befallen me. When the Emperor arrived at the Brandt Sugar Refinery six versts from here, he halted to change his attire and gave fifty ducats to the supervisor as a gift.

Farewell.

J. G. Classen.

Wilhelm Brandt moved to Archangel for the third time in 1820, evidently to build up business even more. His family followed him the year after, arriving in Archangel on 28 May. The house in Othmarschen was shuttered up but remained in the ownership of the family. His main agent in Hamburg, J. C. Meeden, was left to represent the business there. In 1821 he arranged the appointment of schoolmaster Claus Untiedt to Archangel's Evangelical Church School, whose improvement seems to have been a prerequisite for the relocation of the Brandt children. Some years later Mrs Elisabeth Wendeline fell ill, necessitating her return to Hamburg. She left Archangel in the summer of 1826 accompanied by her children Eduard, Elisabeth, Richard and Robert on their own ship the *Elisabeth*

THE STORY OF A FAMILY TRADING COMPANY

The Peter the Great Technical School Building (The Brandt House), Archangel. Built in 1826 as a sugar refinery for Wilhelm Brandt, this imposing stone factory, with its portico and Doric columns, supplied the whole of northern Russia. When the factory closed at the end of the 19th century, the building was converted for use as the Technical School named after Peter the Great. During the Soviet period the Institute for Scientific Research was housed here, but now it is home to the Regional Administrative Department of Justice and the Oktyabrsky Regional Court.

Brandt, but died en route. Two years later Wilhelm concluded a second marriage with Mary Crowe, the daughter of a Russian naval officer of English origin and a German lady from Archangel. This gave the younger children the second mother they so needed. Mrs Mary gave her husband another two sons, but one of them lived for only eighteen months.

In the 1820s, the company of my great-great-great-grandfather established itself in a leading position not only in Archangel but in the entire Russian trading world. They were soon freighting more than 200 ships a year, quite a few of which were the company's own. At the end of the decade their fleet was augmented by a series of vessels named after the victories of the Turkish Wars of 1828–29.

When I was working at the bank which was an eventual offshoot of Wilhelm's activities, we began to finance ships and ship-owners. One of the ways in which we did this was by actually buying the ship, then effectively leasing it to the ship-owner for a period of five or ten years.

Because we were then the registered owner of these vessels, we thought it would be interesting to discover whether Wilhelm Brandt had had a house flag. We wrote to the Russian authorities in Archangel and they wrote back with a complete record of the ships he had owned – about 35 of them – and their movements in and out of the harbour of Archangel. Unfortunately, they had no record of any house flag.

In 1977, at a Jubilee event near our home in Suffolk, we were approached by a lady from Christies who had seen a picture of one of the ships of the Brandt fleet. The painting had come through their auction rooms in the West End, but had not sold. Later she rang and told us that it was now for sale at Sotheby's. My wife and I went, hearts beating, and bought it. The ship was named after his eldest son, Wilhelm Brandt Jnr., and was shown flying the house flag.

Classen set up his own business in the year 1824, whereupon the company assumed once again the name Wm. Brandt.

The sugar factory flourished and secured a market in the whole of northern Russia. They owned a timber yard with a sawmill in Maymaksa on the river Dvina, downstream from the city; the company also owned some ropewalks and a vinegar brewery.

The older sons took up apprenticeships in their father's business. In order to give the eldest of them, Wilhelm, his own sphere of activity, and to exploit opportunities in Petersburg and Baltic trade, Wilhelm Brandt founded a second branch office in Petersburg which was opened by his brother-in-law Karl Amburger, who was given its directorship on 8 February 1827. He, however, died after just a few weeks and the young Wilhelm quickly became fully independent. He was made a partner at Archangel on 1 January 1828 and at Petersburg exactly a year later, whereupon the company was renamed Wilh. Brandt & Sohn in the former city, Wilh. Brandt & Co. in the latter.

Wilhelm Brandt's economic situation in Archangel was excellent, as was his social standing. He became the Consul for Hamburg in 1802 and in 1828 received the title of Consul General for his services. He also represented Bremen. When the house of van Brienen declared bankruptcy

The Stock Exchange, St Petersburg, 1880. Oil painting by Alexander Beggrov (1841–1914). Courtesy of Denis Brandt.

in 1821 (Wilhelm's father-in-law Abraham, the sustainer of the business, had died in 1813), Wilhelm also took over the Dutch consulship from the previous incumbent Abraham Roussatier, a partner in van Brienen; this was done provisionally in 1821 and formalised on 1 July 1822. No fewer than four of his sons held the position of Dutch Consul.

Wilhelm Brandt was especially active in church and school affairs. A Lutheran by birth, he married a member of the Reformed Congregation in Archangel. His sons were baptised in the Lutheran, his daughters in the Reformed Church. He became Church Representative during his first stay there, and in 1816 he was appointed a Church Elder. On Reformation Day in the year 1817, when the Confessions were unified in Prussia, he encouraged a similar union in Archangel, which happened at Easter 1818. Archangel long remained the only unified congregation in Russia. It has already been stated that he appointed the schoolmaster Untiedt. He also provided ample financial support to church and school, as was traditional in the Archangel congregations.

In 1825 he was made *Kommerzienrat*, an honorary title roughly translatable as Councillor of Commerce, and six years later he was elected

The early 19th-century oil painting of the ship reproduced on the front of the book jacket shows the *Wilhelm Brandt Jnr* off the coast of Heligoland. One of the fleet named after members of the family and owned by the company, she traded between Archangel, the Baltic, Africa and the Caribbean.

Stadthaupt, which literally means 'head of the city', an office which entailed a peculiar burden of responsibility on account of the cholera which then raged throughout Russia.

Once his eldest son seemed mature and experienced enough to take over the entire business, Wilhelm called him to Archangel from Petersburg in 1832, whereupon Gustav Brückner, Karl Amburger's son Alexander and the second son of his brother Eduard Brandt took over directorship at Petersburg. Wilhelm himself intended to retire and planned to visit London and his branch office in Hamburg, but while preparing for the journey he became unwell and died after a short illness, on 24 July 1832.

His widow, Mary née Crowe, remained in Archangel where she had grown up and where her own relatives lived, and there reared her son Emanuel Henry and her three youngest stepsons. In later years, when her son was an apprentice, she travelled a great deal. She lost her house in the great fire of Archangel in 1851. In the year 1861 she followed her son to Petersburg and was due to be accommodated at his home in Zurich, where Emanuel moved in 1879. While it was being furnished she stayed in Heilbronn, home of the Kneuper and Condy families whom they knew from Archangel. She died there before her son's household could take her in.

Wilhelm Brandt had ten children from his first marriage: my great-great-grandfather Wilhelm, Alexander, Eduard, Edmund, Elisabeth (Betsey), Adolf, Carl, Gustav, Richard and Robert; and from his second marriage he had two: Julius and Emanuel Henry.

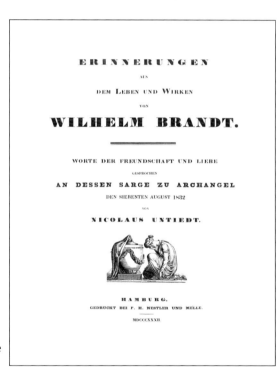

Memories
From
The Life and Working Life
Of
William Brandt
Words of Friendship and Love
Spoken
On this Coffin in Arkangel
7th August 1832
By
Nicolaus Untiedt
Hamburg
Printed by F. H. Nestler and Melle
1832

Emanuel Heinrich Brandt in London
FOURTH GENERATION

Emanuel Heinrich (Henry) Brandt, 1776–1852.

Having so far pursued a strictly linear course down the years, we now need to branch sideways to Wilhelm's older brother, my fourth-great-uncle Emanuel Heinrich Brandt, because it was he who moved to London and set up the Brandt operations there which would subsequently become the family bank.

Emanuel Heinrich (Henry) Brandt was born in Hamburg on 8 March 1776. Mindful of his son's welfare, Emanuel Heinrich's father paid the usual school subscription fee when his son was just two years old; Madame Lambinet also received one such payment in 1779; Mrs Thamsen in 1781. It is probable that these ladies ran some kind of kindergarten. As mentioned previously, Emanuel's brother, my great-great-great-grandfather, was educated by at least one of them. The trainee pastor C. F. Brügmann taught at the house from that year onwards; he later became a pastor in Bergedorf. Two years later Emanuel and Wilhelm were entrusted to Madame Volger and the tutor J. A. Schmidt. The siblings contracted smallpox in the year 1786. In 1789 Albert Angely began to give them lessons in French and in 1792 William Immanuel Tanner of Ipswich taught them English. Emanuel remained with these two tutors up until 1795, even though he had already started as an apprentice at Lubbert & Dumas in 1791.

Wilhelm having returned from his apprenticeship at Archangel in 1798, both brothers took the Citizen's Oath on 26 April 1799. After that they entered the service of Emanuel Jenisch on their fated voyage to the West Indies. Little attention was paid to neutral flags in the bitter naval and trade war carried on at that time between Britain and France. After news of the death of their father arrived, in September 1800, Emanuel requested his release from Jenisch and returned to Hamburg in early November on the ship *Wachsamkeit*, while Wilhelm remained behind.

Emanuel took over his father's business as an insurance broker and, following the death of his mother in 1801, moved to 36 Gröninger Straße in Hamburg. But he enjoyed little success. That is why, in 1805, he and some friends accepted his brother's proposal to move to London as agents for his booming Archangel business. It may well have been that Wilhelm did this in order to avoid the British naval blockade, because his cargoes would then have been consigned through London, making them effectively British shipments. The company Conr. Gottl. Martens & Co. at 28 Jungfernstieg continued to represent Emanuel's interests in Hamburg for some years. And although now in London, he remained linked to Hamburg in other ways; he owned houses there at 1 Neuer Jungfernstieg and 19 Fehlandstraße and donated a significant sum towards victims of the Great Fire of Hamburg in 1842.

In London, he represented his brother's Archangel business under his own name – the beginning of the firm in which I was ultimately involved. They sold what was called 'colonial produce' – cocoa, coffee and

The first cheque issued by Brandts, London, 1812.

sugar. They also traded in a wide variety of other goods including wheat, corn, rice, oats; hemp, flax, flax goods (e.g. linen) and linseed, cotton, button lace, indigo; hides and skins (e.g. calfskins, bearskins), cutch (a vegetable extract containing tannin used for tanning and dyeing), bristles and mats; shellac, iron, potash (used for fertiliser and gunpowder), tallow (animal fats used in candlemaking and soap as well as a wide range of other uses), pitch and tar, as well as wine and cigars. He also represented other businesses, most of them based in Russia. The reputation which the company Wm. Brandt had earned itself in the world served him well. In 1810 he lived at 2 Union Place, City Road; in 1820 at Bloomsbury Square, and in the 1840s he lived at York Terrace and Gloucester Lodge, St. Leonards. He began his business at Batson's Coffee House, which during the previous century had been famous as a gathering-place of physicians. Later he relocated the firm to 34 Lombard Street.

Cheque issued by William Brandt, Archangel, 1812, to E. H. Brandt, Baston's Coffee House.

Following the death of his brother Wilhelm, he realised that his son Adolphus would have no support, so he named his nephew Alexander a partner on 19 October 1832 and called the firm Emanuel Henry Brandt & Co. After that nephew's death in 1838, the third nephew Edmund moved to London and took control of the business. Emanuel Henry then withdrew entirely from the firm at the end of 1839, having changed its name to Emanuel Henry Brandt's Son & Co. Adolphus, however, was merely a partner in name and was not involved in managing things, moving instead abroad, becoming London's Consul General to the Kingdom of Bavaria on 7 December 1847, and living out his later life in Lucerne. Emanuel retained influence over his nephews' affairs even after his retirement; they took his counsel whenever they disagreed.

This left Edmund as the sole director of the London firm, which by then was called Emanuel Henry Brandt's Son & Co. He sent his family several times to spend the summer in Petersburg (1834 and 1848 for example, in which years they took the journey from Hull on their own vessel, *Wilhelm Brandt Jnr.*, a painting of which is mentioned above). In 1851 Edmund himself travelled to Petersburg via Hamburg and in Wiborg took the oath as a Finnish subject. The German Hospital in London was established with his assistance in 1843. In 1854 he had to leave London at the request of the Russian Consul on account of the war between England and Russia. He left the leadership of the business in the hands of his friend Edmund Field and moved to Hamburg. He was not able to return to London until the end of 1855, after which he ran the Brandt's firm until the arrival of his nephew, my great-grandfather, Augustus Ferdinand Brandt, in 1857.

Already in the early 1830s, Emanuel Henry had begun to travel annually to the Continent to visit spa towns and give his wife Susanne Stephanie Sylvestre the opportunity to see her native city of Geneva again. He spent the winter of 1832/33 in the south of France; in 1834 he visited Schlangenbad, Salzburg, Bad Kreuth and Italy; and in 1835 he went to Switzerland where his elder daughter married. In 1841, by which time he was not actively involved in the business, he remained

Emanuel Heinrich (Henry) Brandt.

in Pisa to take the waters; from there he travelled via Hamburg and Travemünde by sea to Russia for the first time to help his nephews bring order to their tangled personal and business affairs. He visited Petersburg, Archangel (where he was celebrated as the brother of Wilhelm Brandt), Moscow and Riga, then returned via Germany. The following year he was in Bad Ems, 1843 in Geneva, 1845 in Geneva and the south of France (La Malou near Montpellier), 1846 in Pau and Wiesbaden. In 1851 he again went to Geneva and Montpellier with his wife and children. There a stomach disorder from which he suffered quickly deteriorated and he died on 11 March 1852. Adolphus brought the body to England. It was buried in Norwood Cemetery, where his wife would also be interred six years later. Emanuel Henry gave generous consideration to various charitable institutions in his will. He was one of the founders of The Society of Friends of Foreigners in Distress.

Mary Espérance Kalm
FIFTH GENERATION

Before returning to the main family line and the main thread of our narrative, we will continue our digression in the line of Emanuel Henry and mention another of his children alongside Adolphus, his remarkable daughter Mary Espérance Kalm Brandt, my first cousin thrice removed.

Mary Espérance was born in Southgate, London, on 8 November 1818 and was named Espérance after her mother's sister and Kalm after her father's foremost employee. She was brought up mainly by her aunt and godmother in Geneva and Rome. Unusually gifted, she amassed considerable knowledge at an early age. Her talent for languages enabled her to acquire a further five languages over the years in addition to the language of her father, mother and country of birth. She was courted

Mary Espérance Kalm, 1818–1899.

by her cousin Alexander Brandt, the eldest son of Wilhelm Brandt in Archangel, while still almost a child. Her father granted her two years' grace, hoping perhaps that this would be ample time for Alexander to realise that his highly-gifted but demanding and volatile cousin, so full of fantastic ideas, could not be the right wife for him, but he went ahead and married her in May 1836. Because of the differences between the spouses and the intellectual superiority of the wife, but also on account of her disregard for the dictates of bourgeois culture, the marriage was very unhappy and ended two years later in Alexander's suicide.

The nineteen-year-old widow then set off on her travels, stopping in Rome and marrying Ferdinand von Schwartz in 1842, whose father had been a childhood friend of Emanuel Henry and who had apprenticed with Brandt in London from 1833 onwards. This enabled her to give free rein to her wanderlust. With her husband she journeyed, mostly by horse, through Greece, European Turkey and Asia Minor and visited Egypt. Most or all of these places would have still been part of the Ottoman Empire, although by then it was in the process of slow disintegration. While on the way to Tunis she was shipwrecked and only rescued by chance.

Her first literary work, a description of this journey entitled *Blätter aus dem afrikanischen Reisetagebuch einer Dame*, was published in 1849.[3] She wrote under the name 'Elpis Melena' (Elpis being a Greek translation of Espérance). She settled in Rome the same year. Her second marriage had brought her no happiness either, so she separated from Ferdinand Schwartz in 1854. Her first novel, *Memoiren eines spanischen Priesters*,[4] was written in Rome in 1857. Her time in that city was punctuated by frequent journeys.

She visited the hero of liberty, Garibaldi, in 1857 on the island of Caprera where he lived in exile. This visit she repeated, which led to a close friendship, and she made certain sacrifices to this end, looking

---

3 Published in English as *Leaves from a Lady's Diary of her Travels in Barbary*.
4 *Memoirs of a Spanish Priest*.

after Garibaldi's children, using her influential ties in Italy for his political aims and caring for him following his wounding and imprisonment. Garibaldi gave her his memoirs in gratitude, which she translated into German and published in 1860 as *Garibaldis Denkwürdigkeiten*. Her relations with Garibaldi, which included his ultimately unsuccessful proposal of marriage, are reflected in various of her own works. 1860 saw the publication of *Hundert und ein Tag auf meinem Pferde. Nebst Besuch auf der Insel Maddalena*,[5] the following year *Blicke auf Calabrien und die Liparischen Inseln im Jahre 1860*,[6] in 1864 *Garibaldi in Varignano 1862 und auf Caprera 1863*,[7] and finally *Garibaldi, Mitteilungen aus seinem Leben*.[8]

At the end of 1865, 'Elpis Melena' settled on the island of Crete where she set up home in the village of Khalepa near Chania, living there until the year 1896 and leaving it to travel only for short periods. Her tireless efforts in service of the local people earned her such popularity throughout the island that she was never once slighted in its constant political turmoil, and her property was never damaged. She founded hospitals, refuges and schools, translated German schoolbooks into modern Greek, and in a book entitled *Kreta-Biene* she translated Cretan folksongs and sayings into German. As well as that she dedicated herself to animal welfare, not only in Crete but extending her activities throughout Europe. She founded a veterinary clinic in Chania. She spoke out about animal welfare and against vivisection in numerous brochures published in several languages. But this was not the only way in which her pen was kept busy. On Crete she wrote: *Der junge Stelzentänzer. Episode während einer Reise durch die westlichen Pyrenäen*[9] (1865), *Die Insel Kreta unter der ottomanischen Verwaltung* (1867),[10] *Von Rom nach Kreta* (1870),[11] the

---

5 *A Hundred and One Days on my Horse. And a visit to the Island of Maddalena.*
6 Published in English as *Calabria and the Liparian Islands in 1860*.
7 *Garibaldi in Varignano 1862 and on Caprera 1863.*
8 Published in English as *Recollections of General Garibaldi.*
9 *The Young Stilt Dancer. Episode on a Journey through the Western Pyrenees.*
10 *The Island of Crete under Ottoman Administration.*
11 *From Rome to Crete.*

novella *Gemma, oder Tugend und Laster*[12] (1877) and *Erlebnisse und Beobachtungen eines mehr als 20 jährigen Aufenthalts auf Kreta* (1892).[13] She left Crete in the year 1896 and moved to Switzerland, where she died just three years later.

---

12 *Gemma, or Virtue and Vice.*
13 *Experiences and observations during more than twenty years on Crete.*

Wilhelm Brandt Jnr.
FIFTH GENERATION

We now rejoin the main narrative with Wilhelm Brandt Jnr., my great-great-grandfather, who was born in Archangel on 25 December 1804. Wilhelm came to Hamburg at the age of two when his parents moved there. During his family's second sojourn in Archangel from 1811 to 1816 he was taught by Seyfert and Oldekop in the Evangelical Church School, after which he returned to Hamburg with his parents and completed his school education. After that he travelled to Archangel with his mother and siblings and entered his father's firm.

In 1827, when his father considered him mature enough for his own activities, he was sent to Petersburg to become the head of a newly established branch, with his uncle Karl Amburger as a mentor. But Amburger

Wilhelm Brandt Jnr., 1804–1857.

Wilhelm Brandt Jnr., 1804–1857.

Pauline Catharina Brandt (née Amburger), 1808–1891.

died just a few weeks later, leaving the 24-year-old reliant upon himself. His management of the business earned his father's approval, and this eldest son was made a partner at Archangel on 1 January 1828 and at Petersburg a year later. Since Wilhelm was from that point on a merchant in Archangel, he was permitted to apply for the position of Danish Consul in that town, even though he was resident in Petersburg. For this he was nominated on 10 March 1830, whereupon he nominated his friend Alexander Amburger, Karl's son, as Vice Consul. He became acquainted with Karl's niece Pauline Amburger at the house of his friend Gustav Brückner, who was married to Karl Amburger's stepsister Juliane; he married Pauline in St. Petersburg on 16 February 1829.

His father hatched a plan to entrust his son with his main business, so Wilhelm Jnr. had to leave Petersburg on 13 March 1832 and hand over the business there to Brückner, his brother Eduard and Alexander Amburger. No sooner had he learned the ropes at Archangel than his father suddenly died. As his successor, he was confronted with the difficult task of guiding the business through the rest of the shipping season while at the same time sorting out the inheritance and looking after his stepmother and siblings. In fact there was so much business that the estate could not be settled until 1839. Wilhelm led the company alone at first, later taking on his brothers Eduard and Edmund as partners in both operations at the end of 1833, whereupon he changed the name of the Archangel business to W. Brandt & Söhne. He then called Eduard to Archangel to assist him while Edmund took over directorship at Petersburg. Alexander Amburger also relocated to work at the Archangel company. The firm's activities were built up and warehouses and agents established all over the north of Russia. The sugar factory was especially profitable, while their own ships provided a subsidising business. Woodlands and sawmills were leased from the state in Onega. Wilhelm Jnr. was made Consul of the Kingdom of Hanover in February 1833. He moved once again to Petersburg in the winter of 1837/38 to expand the company there, leaving the Archangel business under the management of Eduard, at whose side stood his brother Carl and Alexander Amburger. Wilhelm lived first in the 3rd line on Vasily Island, and then purchased Sievers' house in the 10th line to live and do business in; he moved there on 28 September 1840. Gustav Brückner left the company which he had co-directed for three years, and Edmund moved to London in 1838 to replace their deceased brother Alexander. Carl was made a partner in both businesses on 1 January 1840. He was given his own sphere of activity in Riga a year later when they founded a third Russian business, Brandt Gebrüder.

Wilhelm Jnr. was able to attain a respectable position for the Petersburg business, even if it never quite achieved the outright supremacy of the family's Archangel operation. He gradually manoeuvred the firm into the foremost ranks of the city's exporters. He leased the Kussov Sugar Factory from 1844 to 1847. He was nominated as Consul for Hamburg on 8 February 1843 at the suggestion of 67 Hamburg and 18 Petersburg firms; for this he gave up his Danish consulship in Archangel on 19 April; it was bestowed instead upon Alexander Amburger.

From 1840 to 1847 he was a member of the Directorate of the Second Russian Insurance Company, founded in 1835, and, from 1848 to 1853, of the First Transport Comptoir. In 1846 he acquired Finnish citizenship, which had considerable advantages over Russian.

His family, which was expanding almost annually, spent the summer in Ishora near Petersburg, until Wilhelm had built his own house in Pargolovo in 1842.

After Eduard's death in summer 1848, and amid serious disputes between Carl and the other brothers, they decided in 1849 to divide up the whole complex of businesses. Wilhelm together with Edmund (who remained in London) took over the Petersburg business on their own account, while Carl, and Gustav who had been a partner since 1845, became sole proprietors of the company in Riga and Archangel. Alexander Amburger, who had already supported Wilhelm for a year, remained with him as a shareholding *Prokurist*.

Pargola, Finnish House.

Family members at Pargola.

Wilhelm and his wife, together with their eldest son Augustus, embarked upon an extended journey abroad in 1848 which brought them via Paris to London, whence they returned via Holland, the Rhine and Hamburg. In 1851 Wilhelm travelled by himself to Holland and to the Great Exhibition in London. He spent three months of the following year travelling alone while his family met with relatives in Bad Kreuznach, where he collected them after travelling through Switzerland.

By 1851, Alexander Amburger had left because of illness and Eduard Bartelink had replaced him. Business developed very well during the initial years of autonomy, but at the end of 1853 the Crimean War broke out with Turkey, and England and France intervened the following year. Russia's ports were blockaded and trade faltered. Under those circumstances their sizeable business in iron incurred heavy losses, on top of which there were a series of bankruptcies in Petersburg and abroad. Wilhelm became very pessimistic about the future. Despite this he went ahead with a plan which he had earlier made: on 11 May 1854 he sent his wife and most of the children ahead, handed over the business to Bartelink and left Petersburg on 15 May together with his daughters Henriette, Amalie and Minna. They journeyed via Berlin to Hamburg where their country house in Othmarschen had been renovated and comfortably furnished. The family spent the summer at the seaside in Düsternbrook near Kiel. The turbulence of those months and Wilhelm's anxiety about feeding his large and growing family in the event of a collapse in business so impacted his health that he sank into depression. The business was in good hands with Bartelink, but Wilhelm had not given him the kind of autonomy needed when a manager is absent in such periods of war and crisis. Mrs Pauline and Edmund, who had had to leave London during the war, tried to calm the desperate man but to no avail. When the war came to an end and trade picked up again he was desperately needed in Petersburg, yet he could not resolve to

William Brandt Jnr. Portrait by A. Febens, 1854.

Pauline Catharina Brandt. Portrait by A. Febens, 1854.

travel. He spent some time in Dresden with his sister, not returning to Petersburg until April 1856. The shipping season that year had shown how unfounded his anxieties were. Business recovered quickly and the following year the firm achieved third place in turnover among all of Petersburg's companies. But the sorely-tested man did not live to see these happy events. His weakened health finally gave way at the start of the year and he died on 29 January (10 February) 1857. His gravestone at Smolensk Cemetery bears the inscription:

> *Friede Vater sei mit Deiner Asche, Friede*
> *Weinend brachten wir Dich hier zur Ruh'*
> *Deines mühevollen Erdenlebens müde*
> *Eiltest Du der besseren Heimat zu*
> *Mit dem Troste ließest Du die Deinen*
> *Doch im Himmel wird uns Gott vereinen.*

> Peace be with your ashes father, peace
> Tearful we brought you here to rest
> Tired of the trials of life on earth
> You hurried to a home more bless'd
> Thus consoled your loved ones wait:
> God unite us at Heaven's Gate.

Upon receiving news of Wilhelm's death, his eldest son hurried home from Liverpool to be at his mother's side and settle the estate. This, and the settling of their father's estate, must have been further complicated because Russia did not have primogeniture, making entities difficult to hold together, and therein may lie one of the reasons why the Brandt family's once highly-successful Russian activities disappeared around this period.

Mrs Pauline brought up her younger children successfully and with extraordinary vigour. The family spent every summer in Pargolovo. Their town-house gradually became too large as most of the daughters were married off; it was sold around 1870. Pauline Brandt moved to Hamburg in the year 1885 where she spent the remaining years of her life with her eldest son to whom she was very attached. She died on 13 March 1891.

Wilhelm Brandt Jnr. and Pauline had a remarkable progeny with no less than 18 children and 72 grandchildren. Their children were: my great-great-uncles Wilhelm (died in infancy), Walther August (died in infancy), Alexander Nikolaus (died aged 3), Alfred Ernst (no children), and Arthur Henry (who had 5 children); my great-great-aunts Caroline Emilie (who had 6 children), Pauline (Poscha) Elisabeth (2 children), Henriette Sophie (6 children), Mary Hope (9 children), Amalie (Malia) Friederike (no children), Wilhelmine (Minna) Auguste (10 children), Sarah Johanna (no children), Ida Mathilde (10 children), Elisabeth Wendeline (died aged 2), Clara Dorothea (9 children), Emilie (Emmy) Pauline (8 children) and Alida (no children); and my great-grandfather Augustus Ferdinand (who had 7 children).

Augustus Ferdinand Brandt, as a young man.

Augustus Ferdinand Brandt
SIXTH GENERATION

My great-grandfather, Augustus Ferdinand Brandt, was born in Archangel on 22 March 1835. His numerous godparents were Alexander Amburger, Andreas Amburger (his great-uncle), Karl Ludwig Amburger (his uncle), Caroline Amburger née Ketterlinus (his step-grandmother), Marie Weikard née Amburger, Anna Grell wid. Crowe, née Gernet and Nikolaus Untiedt.

Augustus Ferdinand was brought up in Petersburg where he had moved with his parents at the age of two; he was educated together with his friend Eduard Blessig at a private school belonging to one Dr Carl

Augustus Ferdinand Brandt, 1835–1904. Portrait by Carl Johann Lasch, 1883.

May, in whose boarding house he was accommodated; he spent only the weekends with his parents. After that his education continued at the *Höhere Kommerzpension*.[14] In 1848 he accompanied his parents abroad and got to know Paris, London, Holland and several German towns and cities. In Holland he visited Peter the Great's cottage in Zaandam, a blacksmith's wooden hovel where the Tsar had stayed in 1697 while visiting Holland incognito. In its visitors' book, Augustus Ferdinand was astonished to find entries made by both his grandfathers, who, without knowing each other, had visited the same place in the same year, 1802. The cottage still stands today.

Augustus Ferdinand began his commercial apprenticeship with his father in Petersburg. He travelled with the whole family to Hamburg via Berlin in May 1854, and from there, on 26 May 1855, as soon as it was permitted for him as a Finnish subject, he went over to England. There he worked for a short time at Schuster Son & Co. in London, but because that placement gave him little opportunity to learn, he went just a few months later to Liverpool and entered the large trading organisation of Blessig Braun &. Co. which was in close business relations with the Brandt companies. There he gained a fatherly friend in his employer Francis Caesar Braun, who appointed him his executor before his death in 1873.

Augustus Ferdinand's father died in early 1857, so he had to go to Petersburg in February to settle the estate together with managing director Bartelink. The 22-year-old was given *Prokura*, or general commercial power of representation, on 20 February. No further changes were made until the heirs had been taken care of. In London, however, the widow and uncle Edmund appointed young Augustus a partner on 1 July, whereupon the company name was shortened from Emanuel Henry Brandt's Son & Co. to E. H. Brandt's Son & Co. He became a partner in the Petersburg business at the end of 1858. But, on the advice of his friend Braun, he did not remain in Russia; he decided instead to

---

14   A college of commerce.

work at the London branch, from which his uncle Adolphus resigned around the same time. He immediately changed the name, to William Brandt, Sons, and Company. Emanuel Henry, the brother of his father William Brandt Junior, had no descendants in the firm any more, and because William Brandt Senior was his grandfather and Emanuel Henry's father, he justified this new name by saying: "We are all the sons of William Brandt."

Augustus Ferdinand Brandt persuaded his uncle Edmund to move to Petersburg, which meant that he alone remained the sole director of what was at that time still a modest London merchant business, nothing more than an agency for the Petersburg firm. Only later did it develop into one of London's leading banking houses which I myself would end up directing. For now it was just a typical little German bank, but operating in England. Records that still exist show the notes the partners wrote to each other in German. But they traded and banked around the world. Their clients were mainly in North America, South America, and on the Continent. They had very few British clients, unlike many of London's other merchant banks, who became very much part of the British Establishment, having leading British firms among their clientele. Like many of those merchant banks, William Brandt's transformed its merchanting business gradually, putting their names on the bills of other merchants whose business they understood and thus becoming an Accepting House. The security was always in the goods which the merchant was trading in.

In 1863 Augustus Ferdinand married Elisabeth (Lilly) Oesterreich, daughter of the merchant, later Chancellery Director at the Ministry of Finance in St. Petersburg, Constantin August Oesterreich and his wife Marie Elisabeth Prehn.

He had been fortunate to survive the collapse of his uncle Carl's business in 1861, and in 1865 dissolved his ties to the Petersburg headquarters, although he continued to represent it until its liquidation in 1878, just as he continued to represent E. H. Brandt & Co. in Petersburg and Archangel up until 1885.

Elisabeth Brandt (née Oesterreich), 1835–1922. Portrait by Carl Johann Lasch, 1883.

Shortly after taking over the London business, he took on his brother-in-law Hermann Loehnis as a partner. Loehnis had been an independent merchant in New York before marrying Augustus Ferdinand's older sister Henriette Sophie and moving to London to join the firm. He left again at the end of 1877, taking a capital sum of £54,000 which he had earned there, and spent the rest of his years in Bonn and Berlin. Augustus Ferdinand appointed his brother Alfred Ernst Brandt as a partner in 1876 and his youngest brother Arthur Henry in 1880. The former died in 1895, having spent his final two years in Davos with a lung complaint; the latter left at the end of 1898 and set up his own business called Arthur H. Brandt & Co, dying much later, in 1923. The only constant at the London firm was Augustus Ferdinand himself.

The state of my great-grandfather's health (the early stages of a disease of the spinal cord) compelled him, on the advice of his doctors, to leave London in 1880; he chose to settle in Hamburg. Despite this, he retained a firm hold on the overall directorship of the business up until his death. He made his two eldest sons Augustus Philip and Henry Bernhard partners on 1 January 1895, and the third son Rudolph Ernst on 1 January 1899. These were the great-uncles I would later come to know so well. His youngest son, my grandfather, did not enter the business at all.

My great-grandfather, after leaving London, lived in Hamburg at 1 Neue Rabenstraße. He purchased Villa Testorp in Nienstedten on the Elbe as a summer residence in the year 1888, some miles downstream from the old Brandt residence in Othmarschen. This property, which he called Villa Brandt, later became the permanent home of his youngest son Ludwig Walther, my grandfather, the first of his generation whom I came to know personally.

Augustus Ferdinand was condemned to spend the last fifteen years of his life a complete physical cripple despite perfect presence of mind. He died in Hamburg on 24 January 1904 and was buried at Nienstedten four days later. From the small agency he took over in 1857 with a staff of just six employees, he had created, over the course of a life dedicated entirely to work, a first-rate banking house, which was our family firm, and from the £10,000 bequeathed to him by his father he left an estate of over one million pounds.

Hamburg, Neue Rabenstraße 1.

WM. BRANDT'S SONS & CO.

Hamburg, Neue Rabenstraße 1. Interior.

Portrait of Augustus Ferdinand and Elisabeth's children, taken to commemorate their Silver (25th) Wedding Anniversary in 1888. *Left to right – Standing:* Rudolf (Rudie) Ernst Brandt, Elisabeth (Lilly) Pauline Goverts (née Brandt), Henry Bernhard Brandt; *Seated:* Augustus Philip Brandt, Ludwig (Louis) Walther Brandt, Marie Schramm (née Brandt).

Villa Brandt, Nienstedten.

Augustus Ferdinand Brandt.   Elisabeth Brandt (née Oesterreich).

Augustus Ferdinand and his wife had seven children: Wilhelm, who died aged four, Marie, Elisabeth (Lili) Pauline, Augustus (Gussy) Philip, Henry Bernhard, Rudolph (Rudi) Ernst, and my grandfather Ludwig (Louis) Walther.

Ludwig Walther Brandt
SEVENTH GENERATION

My grandfather Ludwig Walther Brandt, Anglicised as Louis Walter and known as Louis to all but my grandmother, was born in London on 15 November 1875. He moved with his parents to Hamburg in autumn 1880 where he attended a prep school run by Adolf Thomsen, then the Johanneum Grammar School and a private school run by Dr Theodor August Bieber. His apprenticeship was at F. M. Wolff from 1892 to 1895.

Stammbuch (family book/album), page 3.

In summer 1895, he boarded with Pastor Goetz at Geneva, and from 1895 to 1897 he was employed at our bank in London, Wm. Brandt's Sons & Co. He travelled the Far East in 1897–98, visiting Japan, China, Manila, the Dutch East Indies, and then the Straits Settlements, Burma and British India.

He did not return to join his older brothers running the bank as might have been expected. Perhaps there was no room in it, and he did not want to be under their thumb. Instead, my grandfather began in 1899 to work at Alex Oetling & Co. in Hamburg in the hope of being taken on there, and in 1901 he travelled on their behalf through the United States to Mexico, Ecuador, Peru, Chile, Argentina, Uruguay and Brazil. He then became a partner in Alex Oetling & Co. from 1901 to 1914. Because he was a British citizen, the Great War put a stop to this work. He was interned in a camp at Ruhleben near Berlin from November 1914 to April 1915. It was not until 1921 that he was able to establish his own import and export company in Hamburg, L. W. Brandt & Co. From 1921 to 1929 he also had an office in London under the name L. Brandt & Co together with Cornelius Otto Schütt, the son of his cousin Wilhelm Schütt, as a partner.

He married a Hamburg girl called Louise Merck, known as Lili, on 15 November 1901. My grandmother was the daughter of the Syndic, Dr. jur. Carl Hermann Jasper Merck and his wife Magdalena Meyer. One of her brothers became a senator and all her family were quite artistic. She used to come over to England often. When my parents went on holiday, which they did once or twice a year, she would arrive from Hamburg, live in our house and look after me. There she would write stories for me. She was an extremely warm and friendly lady.

One Christmas I visited my grandparents in Hamburg and they put on a play she had written. Travelling to them in Hamburg was a great adventure. It must have been at the time that my brother was born; perhaps my parents wanted me out of the way. I was six years old and went with my governess to Southampton. The ship did not come alongside the dock; instead we took a tender out to her. She was

The Hamburg office in action.

a Hamburg America Line ship, going from New York to Hamburg and stopping in England on the way. We must have been a night or two on board.

Hamburg is about forty miles up the river Elbe. At the mouth of the Elbe is a small port called Cuxhaven where we disembarked and were met by my grandfather's chauffeur, who drove us to the house, Villa Brandt, in Nienstedten, a riverside suburb of Hamburg. After the death of my grandfather's mother, it had been transferred into his ownership according to his father's will; his three older brothers were all established as partners in London by that time. It was a large, over-furnished, very Victorian, slightly dark house, and not especially beautiful. There were all sorts of staff.

When we arrived from Cuxhaven they said, "Quickly, quickly, run into the garden." The house was right on the river. We went into the garden, and there in the twilight, ablaze with lights, was the ship we had sailed on, with her twin funnels, gliding past our house.

THE STORY OF A FAMILY TRADING COMPANY

Ludwig Walther Brandt, 1875–1965.　　Lili Brandt (née Louise Merck), 1879–1949.

My grandmother devoted a lot of time and attention to us when she visited us in London. One of the family jokes was that she invariably lost her luggage on the way there. She would arrive at our house in Melbury Road and within about half an hour, she would be saying to my father, "Oh, Walter, I've left my suitcase in such-and-such a place." But it invariably turned up. This habit was clearly a feature of her life, because in one of the plays that were put on in Hamburg, they had a joke about her having lost something on her travels.

In June 1939, my grandparents reluctantly left Hamburg after years of pleas from his sons and brothers, who reminded him of how he had spent a part of the previous war. Louis Brandt retired to England, where he lived first in Crawley at a house called Winswood, then at Micheldever House near Winchester in Hampshire. He left his Hamburg business in the hands of his *Prokuristen*, who went on to run it in their names, Fischer & Kniath.

We used to go to this house at Micheldever quite often. My grandmother died there on 9 November 1949. I was only 18 years old at the

53

time; I would have known her much better if she had lived another ten years. After her death, my brother and I would go down and stay there with our grandfather. It was a very attractive Regency building, with a lovely layout and rooms, and the whole setting was pleasant with a wonderful garden. The sun always seemed to be shining. The house was not far from the main railway line down to Southampton, which, of course, still had steam operated trains. My brother and I were steam enthusiasts and we used to spend a lot of time walking the dog in the fields beside the railway track, watching the trains.

My grandfather had been around the world as a young man, and when I came back from my world trip (more of which later), we discussed it. I talked about South America in 1957, he described South America in 1900. I said, "Tremendous future in South America," and he replied, "So was there when I was there in 1900." It had not changed. But none of the future had been realised, and it still is not being realised.

Of his import and export business in Hamburg, L.W. Brandt and Company, he told me once, "I sold a complete church to a town in South Brazil." There are a lot of Germans in South Brazil. The whole church was built in Hamburg and dismantled – pews, organ, altar, steeple – the whole thing. Everything went out and was rebuilt.

My grandfather was always slightly Victorian and stiff, but he was very friendly and always pleased to see us, and also quite lonely. He died in 1965, so for 15 years he lived alone.

Louis and Louise Brandt had four children: my father Walter Augustus and my uncles Hermann Wilhelm (Bill), Rudolf (Rolf) Alexander and Augustus (Gustus) Ludwig.

Walter Augustus Brandt
EIGHTH GENERATION

My father, Walter Augustus Brandt, was born in Hamburg on 7 December 1902. There he attended a preparatory school run by Gustav Bertram and the Heinrich-Hertz-Realgymnasium, from which he graduated by taking the school leaving examination. So although he lived his adult life in England, he was brought up in Germany. Much later, in 1956, when I myself was training in Hamburg, he went back to visit, and he and I went round to the various banks and business houses in Hamburg. We were invited out to dinner every single night he was there, and he had an uproariously good time. I saw a different side of him from the one I knew, because he was actually back home, speaking German, his native

Walter Augustus, Hermann Wilhelm (Bill), Rudolf Alexander (Rolf), Augustus Ludwig (Goo-Goo).

tongue, even though he spoke perfect English. There were lots of jokes and a lot of laughter with his old Hamburg friends, and reminiscences about his childhood and the things he had done.

One such anecdote was about a girl called Berthe-Maria. Her mother was my grandmother's sister, Emily Schroeder, who lived with her family in Schleswig-Holstein. At Christmas time they always came to stay with my grandfather, my father and his brothers in Hamburg. As they were all filing into dinner on the first night, my father, around ten at the time, pinched Berthe-Maria's bottom. Later that night, my grandfather appeared in my uncle Bill's room and accused him of having done this deed. Bill knew nothing about it, but he'd been standing next to her and she thought it was him. There was something of a crisis between the two families, because the perpetrator had degraded himself. Much later, it came out that it had been my father. He told this story with great hilarity, in the presence of Berthe-Maria, by this time aged 55.

After leaving school, my father had spent three months in Lausanne to perfect his French. He began an apprenticeship at Oesterreich & Co. in Hamburg in 1921, moving in 1923 to the family bank in London, Wm. Brandt's Sons & Co., where he worked initially until 1926. In April that year, continuing the family tradition, he set off on a voyage around the world which lasted eighteen months. He spent approximately nine months in South America, then one month in the United States, where he met up with his cousin Henry Augustus Brandt in San Francisco; he travelled with him for nine months through Japan, China, Indochina, the Malay States, Java, Sumatra, Siam, Burma and British India.

It was on that tour, on a boat somewhere between China and Singapore, that he met my mother, Dorothy Gray Crane. She was working at the time for the Dean of the American University in Peking, having left America where she was born, never to live there again and rarely to return – apart from when her mother was ill and dying, and with my father on business trips. After they met, she made her way through India, where she lived near Lucknow for a while, then came to England and married my father in 1929. It was to be a happy marriage.

Dorothy Gray Crane, 1899/1903?–1978.   Walter Augustus Brandt, 1902–1978.

I was later warned against such travelling romances. One of our German cousins had the most delightful mother, Tante Nadia. I used to go and have tea with her. She spoke German with a Russian accent. Knowing I myself was about to go around the world, as my father had before me, she told me, "My dear Peter, travelling acquaintances are dangerous. Be careful!" I protested that my parents had met on a ship. "Ah," she replied, "they were lucky."

My mother may not have gone back to her home country very much, but she did talk about it. Her grandfather had been a banker too, and was obviously a very kind man, because in the various crises through which people go, he had a huge number of mortgages, and could have taken over vast areas of land in America, but he was too good-hearted to foreclose on the mortgages. But perhaps he had another side, because there was another event in which the men from the town came to tar and feather him. Quite why, I don't know. They warned him they were coming, and he escaped and hid on the prairies. My mother would go often, she said, to her grandmother's house, sit in the attic, look out over the garden and countryside, and read Walter Scott. She was quite romantic and a great reader.

My mother ensured that I too learned to love reading. She devoted a huge amount of time and attention to me and my brother. Her father had been a professor of mining engineering at Pennsylvania State University, but I never knew much about him. She obviously adored him and thought he was marvellous. I was rather sad she never went back and saw him for any length of time before he died, which was in 1947. I once asked her why she left America. I think she was in a small-town situation and wanted to escape from it. She must have missed it in her heart of hearts. But I also think, later, she missed China and Eastern philosophies much more than she missed America. She had spent a lot of time studying the Eastern religions, which had had a very strong influence on her while she was living there. She had two sisters younger than her who had stayed on in America. She continued to be close to them, writing frequently.

My father returned to London after his world tour, joined the bank in September 1927 and was made a partner on 1 January 1931, leaving only when the bank was sold in 1972.

It may have been on account of his artistic mother that my father had a very good eye for pictures. At the beginning of the Second World War, he began to buy the British modern painters – John Piper, Henry Moore and others, which were cheap then in modern terms: ten pounds for a Piper, fifteen or so for a Henry Moore. They began to appear on the walls where we were living, which was near Banbury. My mother gave him a great deal of support in doing that. Later, he stopped buying modern British painters and built up a big collection of 18th-century British watercolours. She and he would work together in their little studio, where he had them all stored, cataloguing them. I still have some of them today.

My father did have close friends outside the family, but the difficulty was perhaps that he was brought up entirely in Germany as a German

Walter Augustus Brandt. Portrait by William Coldstream, 1962–3.

boy. He went to German schools and spoke only German until he learned English at school. The society in which he then found himself, when he moved to London – merchant banking – was very much part of the British Establishment and very British in character. He may have felt himself an outsider. It is a notably difficult gap to bridge. He deliberately undertook to absorb that character.

That is not to say that my father felt himself a German national either. His father was British, after all, and was born in England, and other ancestors, although German, had long ceased to be tied to Germany geographically. His grandfather, Augustus Ferdinand, had been born in Archangel, in the German community there, had acquired Finnish nationality, and had moved to London as a twenty-year-old man, only moving to Hamburg in old age. With my father, I think another part of it was that he wanted to swim with the tide. He considered himself British. Far from having split loyalties during the War, he worked for the British Government in the Ministry for Economic Warfare. Owing

Interior of Augustus Philip Brandt's House, Castle Hill, where Philip de László set up his studio, 1928.

to his commitment to the Official Secrets Act, we never managed to extract from him the exact nature of this work. I have met a number of friends of his who worked down the passage from him. I once asked one of them, a man called Anthony Wrightson, what my father actually did during the War. He avoided the issue. He simply said, "I'll tell you a story. One afternoon or evening, I heard a great shout of laughter come out of your father's room. I went in and said, 'Walter, what's happened?'" My father would do broadcasts to the German nation. This was in 1944, when things were getting really difficult in Germany. They sent out a broadcast that Goering was still eating butter. They went on putting this out, over and over again, to try to demoralise the German people by saying that their leaders were living it up while they were all suffering. The occasion for my father's glee was when the German High Command issued a denial on the radio and said that it was not true that Goering was still eating butter.

#

Walter Augustus Brandt.

Walter and Dorothy Brandt.

There is more about my father further on in this account, as most of what I know about him is in the story of my own life. He had two sons: Denis William and me, Peter Augustus.

German Order of Merit awarded to Walter Brandt for services to the Anglo-German Society.

Peter Augustus Brandt
NINTH GENERATION

Birth, Immediate Family

I was born in London on 2 July 1931. My parents were living in Addison Gardens at the time. Later, we lived at Woodland House, which was a wonderful building on Melbury Road by the corner of Holland Park. It had a lovely garden and spacious rooms. I had a huge nursery, so big that I could ride a bicycle in it. I set up soldiers and trains there. The house had been built by an architect called Richard Norman Shaw for the painter Luke Fildes, one of the Leighton group of artists, who lived in it from 1877 until his death in 1927, not long before we moved in. After the War, it was purchased by the father of the film director Michael Winner, who lived there from 1972 until he died in 2003, after which it was bought by a pop star. At some point it got turned into flats, one of which – previously my mother's bedroom – was occupied by an acquaintance whom I once visited. Next door was another interesting property, Tower House, which was lived in after 1962 by John Betjeman, more of whom later.

I retained a connection with that part of London for many years, even after Woodland House went out of the family. When Liza and I were first married, we lived on Holland Villas Road, and when we sold that to spend more time in the country, we bought a house in Kensington Place as a pied-à-terre for when we had to be in the city.

I was the first child. My brother Denis was born five and a half years later. He and I had a very close childhood, probably precisely because of the difference in age. There was little competition and we always got on very well together. We shared many of the same interests and enthusiasms. I look back on it as being an uneventful and perfectly happy childhood.

I had a super nanny for the first three or four years of my life, but oddly enough I do not remember her particularly. Then my carers began to change quite a lot. When my brother was born, there did begin to be a certain amount of rivalry, because the nanny was there for him and not me. I had a governess as well, but at the same time I was going to school.

The first school I went to, when I was four or five, was called Glendower. After that I went to Wagner's. That I do remember, probably because I was quite well-taught there. My mother used to take me. Before I went, she carefully imparted the alphabet to me – "A B C D E F G". Later, on one occasion, my mother was sitting at the back of the class and they pointed to a letter and asked me, "What is that?" And I said, "A", pronouncing it as a long A. They replied, "No, A" – pronouncing it phonetically. I looked round at my mother in frank disbelief, as if she had completely misled me.

At home we had a wonderful parlour maid called Ellen. It was altogether well-staffed; this was still well before World War II and things were quite comfortable. I think we had a scullery maid and a kitchen maid. There must have been a house maid as well. All of them were in uniform. I spent quite a bit of time in the pantry, being given titbits and talking to them.

We also had a gardener. For a time we had a butler, but it was not a great success and he did not stay long. Our gardener gave me all his cigarette cards, which I still possess.

My parents liked entertaining and gave a lot of dinner parties. We would sometimes stand on the stairs and watch the guests arrive. My mother was a great one for generating social activity. She had known nobody when she arrived in England, so she joined the American Women's Club and immediately had a wide circle of friends, mainly British couples where the wives were American.

She familiarised us with books. She would read to me for about half or three-quarters of an hour before I went to bed, which were memorable occasions. We read all the *Swallows and Amazons* books. When she

Dorothy Brandt reading with Peter and Denis.

read *David Copperfield*, she and I wept copiously as the young protagonist was ill-treated.

My mother also told us a lot about the history of her home country – Abraham Lincoln and such like. She came up with all sorts of little snippets and events. She would sing negro spirituals: *Old Black Joe* and suchlike, before we went to bed. We had a lot of American books – *Brer Rabbit* and other American children's tales. As a child, she used to go and stay with her grandparents in the summer. She told us how she would sit upstairs in their house in the loft reading Walter Scott and look out over the countryside. She also mentioned going West during the summer, on which journey the locomotive hooted during the night.

We had a lot of fun with my father as well as my mother. I remember the games, and Saturday afternoons. In the winter, he would come into the nursery after tea and we would play with trains together. But at the same time, he could be somewhat dictatorial and had a much more austere relationship with me than he did with my younger brother, who was the baby. He used to try and discipline Denis over things, but it never really worked. They ended up in each other's arms in tears. In a way I minded this disparity, in another way I did not. I found it rather amusing and never resented it.

My father gave me a lot of support. When I began to row at Eton, to my surprise, when I looked up, after going past the winning post, he would be standing there in his dark suit, having come down from the City to watch the race. I never knew when he was coming.

We played charades and games of that kind. My father was a great one for acting. He was frightfully good at making up French accents and things of that kind. He spoke fluent French, but in this case it was

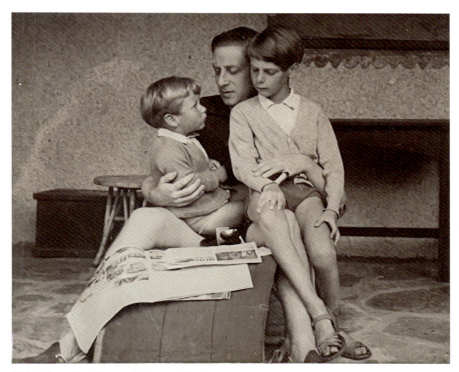

Walter Brandt with sons Peter and Denis.

garbled words which sounded like French. He shrugged his shoulders and behaved exactly like an emotional Frenchman.

His relationship with me may have been austere, but that should not imply that he was a severe person as such. There was a lot of laughter, especially with my mother. And I got closer to my father in the final days of William Brandt's, when we were in conflict with National and Grindlays, the main shareholders, about the way it should be run, and in the ultimate sale of William Brandt's. That brought us together.

Wider Family

At Christmas, our family would drive down and stay at Capenor, which was Great-Uncle Henry's house in Nutford. There were large numbers of other cousins: at least six others of my generation, and there were Henry Brandt's three children, their husbands and wives, and a few other people who were ex-Russian relatives who came and stayed. There were quite a few from the Baltic States, some Estonians who had come to England and were looked after by Great-Uncle Henry and Great-Uncle Augustus.

In the afternoon, as it got dark, Father Christmas would arrive. The house, a splendid Victorian mansion,[15] had a long drive and all the children from the other great-uncle's house, Castle Hill, a mere mile away, would assemble at Capenor. We would wait, tense with excitement. A bell would be heard ringing outside. One year it snowed; it must have been about 1938. Father Christmas (it was one of the great-uncles) came up the drive with a huge sack on his back, stomping through the snow. There was a big hall where we all were. He pulled the things out of the sack and asked us if we had behaved well in the past year, and we were given our presents.

Then, in their drawing room, Great-Uncle Henry and Great-Auntie Lili had a table set out for each child, and on the table were placed the

---

15   Now called Robert Denholm House.

presents we had been given. They were marvellous givers of gifts. The most memorable one I got was an enormous Meccano set, which probably kept me busy for the subsequent ten years. Great-Auntie Lili was a particularly good present giver. I still treasure things she gave me, either before the War or just after. One was a very nicely-made leather box for carrying sandwiches on a horse. The other was a flask, also for attaching to the saddle – glass, a silver top with my initials, and a leather case.

Having had Christmas Day with Great-Uncle Henry, on Boxing Day, we would go over to Great-Uncle Augustus and do the same sort of thing all over again.

I remember those pre-War Christmases very well. There was a lovely, sweet old lady called Auntie Maggie – Margareta Favarger, whose first marriage, in 1879, had been to Alfred Ernst Brandt, the brother of my great-grandfather. She would come and have tea with us on Christmas Eve. The fire would be roaring and we had little tables beside us. I sat neatly on the sofa in my velvet trousers and buckled shoes. Under the Christmas tree were the presents. I was not allowed even to touch them until after this special tea. Auntie Maggie would come, then I would open my presents. My parents would then have dinner together, quietly. I was young and went to bed.

We did not have much contact with these relatives throughout the rest of the year. They came and saw my parents occasionally. But there were exceptions, and one of them was Conny Schutt. He lived in London and often used to have tea with us on Sundays. He was very Russian. He played the piano and sang Russian songs.

His ancestral connection to the Brandts was convoluted and involved three Corneliuses, of which he was the third. My great-great-aunt Caroline Emilie, sister of Augustus Ferdinand, had married, in Russia, Eduard Schütt, Conny's grandfather. The Schütts were wine growers and merchants in the Crimea. But Eduard's father, Cornelius Otto Schütt, was himself a son of an elder Cornelius Otto Schütt and Anna Margaretha Cunitz, making him a grandchild of Anna Margaretha Brandt, the second daughter of Jacob Brandt, who was a son of the Paul Brandt with whom this book begins. Eduard Schütt was therefore his wife's fourth cousin, meaning we were related to his children Conny and Tamara by two different and disparate routes.

Conny's sister Tamara, when she was 23, met a young naval lieutenant called Leslie Haliburton Ashmore, the recently appointed British Naval Intelligence Officer in Sevastopol. It was 1918 and the Bolsheviks were encircling the city. Their courtship in those stormy days was a well-known story in the family. Here is Ashmore's own account, from his book *Forgotten Flotilla*:

> Times did not lend themselves to long courtships. On a visit in February 1919, I proposed to Tamara and was accepted. My impatience to be married found an ally in the Russian church calendar. Lent was due to begin in little more than a week, after which no weddings would be possible until after Easter. It left little time in which to make arrangements. The Zs [i.e. the Schutts] could fix the religious side of things with the priest of the little church of Balaclava. But, as a naval officer, I was in duty bound to seek the approval of my senior officer. In the long run I could not be prevented from marrying whom I wished, but disapproval of my plans might delay them. There were two authorities to placate or circumvent, Colonel Temple back in Constantinople and the senior naval officer at Sevastopol, commanding the British cruiser in the harbour, whom I will call Captain X.
>
> Returning to Sevastopol on the Monday morning, I decided to wait until the weekly mail destroyer had left, which I felt would take care of any possibility of Temple taking a hand. I then made my way aboard the cruiser. Captain X, I knew, was a relic of an age that regarded all foreigners as inferior. He was apt to express his contempt for them in scathing terms, although I fancy he knew few personally. I guessed that I was in for a sticky time.
>
> I was ushered into his cabin by the Officer of the Watch and for a time we spoke of local affairs, finally coming to the question of arrangements for the evacuation of a New Zealand lady married

to a Russian. The conversation, which I remember so well after all these years, was the acme of embarrassment on both sides.

"Mrs ……………'s passage is arranged in the SS ……………, Ashmore. You had better let her know when you go ashore."

"Very well, sir," I replied. "I presume her husband goes with her?"

"Certainly not. We can't be responsible for these damned Russians."

"Well, I don't think she'll go without him, sir," I protested. "I really think we must fix up for both of them to travel or there'll be trouble."

X stared at me for a moment with a look of genuine astonishment on his face and, in a wondering tone, said, "How the devil can such a person marry one of these yellowbellies?"

I had no answer to this odd remark and silence fell between us. Before X could commit himself and embarrass me further, I decided to leap into the fray. "May I bring up a personal matter, sir?"

"Certainly, Ashmore. What is it?"

Drawing a deep breath, I plunged. "I feel I should tell you, sir, that I am intending to marry a Russian girl in five days' time."

I need not have feared that embarrassment on account of his previous remark would silence the gallant Captain for long. Far from it. After glaring at me for a moment, he said, "Well, I would have you know that I do not approve of international marriages. Always unsatisfactory. Besides, I hope you realise that although your Russian friends may have plenty of paper money here, it is quite valueless outside this country."

I thought it was time I left before X tried to forbid my marriage. As I got up to go, I said, "I wonder if you would care to lunch with me the day after tomorrow at the hotel, sir?"

"No, thank you, Ashmore, I'm afraid I can't," he replied. "To meet your fairy, I suppose," he grinned rather sourly.

"Yes, sir. It is to meet the girl I am going to marry," I said, and turned to leave. As I reached the door of his cabin, he called me back. "Well, perhaps I'll be able to make it after all. I'll see."

With that I left, my duty done, and hoped to hear no more of the matter. To my surprise, at luncheon on the day I had named, X duly arrived. Poor X! Tamara made havoc of his fixed determination to dislike all foreigners. Luncheon over, he lingered on and on, entranced, and we had the greatest difficulty in getting rid of him.

Captain X's brusque and boorish manner no doubt hid the proverbial heart of gold, for that evening he made amends with a note brought to me by his coxswain.

"Dear Ashmore," it read. "I should very much like to come to your wedding if you feel like asking me after all that has occurred."

Come he did. On arrival at the church I was shocked to see him standing on the steps, duly rigged in uniform and sword, puffing a pipe. No doubt he felt that this was a suitable gesture of disdain for so un-English a ceremony as a Russian wedding. Certainly he must have been horrified by the elaborate ritual, with the four groomsmen, Djvoritsky, Tchirikoff, Cornelius and a Colonel Baron Nolken, holding the crowns over our heads while the bearded priest intoned. The little church of Balaclava was packed with curious countryfolk besides our own friends. As we left after the reception for our honeymoon, the priest wished us Godspeed. A year later we grieved to hear that the good man was dead at the hands of the Bolsheviks.

Leslie and Tamara Ashmore and Tamara's father and brother were later evacuated. Leslie and Tamara lived in England and had two sons, whom we knew as children. Both of them became important figures in the Navy. Edward Ashmore became Admiral of the Fleet and Chief of Defence Staff in a caretaker role in February 1977, following the death of his predecessor. Peter Ashmore was Master of the Household to HM the Queen, 1973–86, in charge of protocol.

Conny Shutt, his surname by then and perhaps earlier divested of its umlaut, thus ended up living in England and coming to tea with us.

Sir Edward Ashmore, Admiral of the Fleet, 1977, and Chief of the Defence Staff, 1977–79.

Vice Admiral Sir Peter Ashmore, Master of the Household to HM the Queen, 1973–86.

Shortly after the Revolution, having escaped Russia, he went back into St. Petersburg, or Leningrad as it was by then, disguised as a tugboat hand, collected all his family's papers and memorabilia, and got out.

Great-Uncle Augustus took Leslie and Tamara Ashmore's young sons under his wing. They said that if it had not been for his patronage, they would never have had the education they did; an ordinary naval lieutenant did not have enough money to educate his children well. They were both educated at Yardley Court and the Royal Navy College, Dartmouth.

The Ashmores were very much part of family life and were always at the great-uncles' houses at Christmas. They were very glamorous young men. Edward was twelve years older than me, Peter ten years. As a six-year-old, I used to look up to these handsome young relatives. They used to do conjuring tricks that enthralled us all. They were our heroes.

Another notable personality of my childhood was Olga Gütschow. Her husband, Arthur, was a descendent of William Brandt Jnr. and therefore a distant cousin; they had fled Russia in 1920 and come to London. He died the year after I was born, but she lived on until I was 14. She would stay with Great-Uncle Henry and was known as Cousin Olga. I always had to be presented to her in Capenor's huge drawing room. Cousin Olga had a lorgnette. She sat at the far end of the room and I would be taken in to meet her. About half way across the room, the lorgnette would rise to her eyes and I knew I was in focus.

My mother used to tell us how one day, she had been sitting at the dining table next to Great-Uncle Henry, and Cousin Olga was sitting opposite. The settings were generally quite formal. Great-Uncle Henry would be sitting at one end of the table, Great-Auntie Lili at the other, and there would probably be twenty sitting down to lunch. Cousin Olga, as far as I know, never smiled or laughed much. She was not a particularly outgoing person. My mother, eating her lunch, came across a caterpillar in a lettuce leaf, and with one eye on Great-Uncle Henry, she succeeded in manoeuvring the little creature without him noticing, so that it was hidden from view. When she had finished, she looked up and noticed the lorgnette, focused on her salad plate. It was the first time she saw Cousin Olga smile.

Great-Auntie Lili was German. Born Alida Knauer, she was quite a domineering, powerful lady. She would laugh, and her voice would ring out through the house. At the beginning of the Second World War, she received evacuees from London. They came from the East End and were used to putting large quantities of vinegar on their food. They all sat down, she at the head of the table, and they asked for some. She said, "There's no vinegar, and nobody's putting vinegar on my food." There was a bit of a hunger strike for a few meals. But she won in the end.

The grandchildren of Great-Uncle Henry used to come and stay with us from time to time, but we were not particularly close. We played together. For a while I was quite close to a sister, who was slightly older than me. Later I became close to my second cousin John. We worked together in the firm; he did the timber and I ran the bank.

The Uncles

Uncle Bill

My father, like his father before him, had three brothers: William – known as Bill – Rudolf, and Augustus. Bill Brandt was entirely uncommercial, but very artistic and became a renowned photographer. He was great fun and a super uncle. Once, he and my grandfather arrived at the house in Holland Park. I was sitting at my nursery window, looking out, and he picked up clods of earth from the rose bed and threw them at the window, where they exploded. "Black snowballs!" he declared. To me, aged five or six, he was thrilling. I used to spend quite a lot of time with Uncle Bill. During the War we often went down to my grandfather's near Crawley, and Uncle Bill was frequently there.

He also went to Great-Uncle Henry's, where one of the maids was called Pratt. She features a lot in Uncle Bill's photographs, because he did a series of the English at home showing the contrast between big houses with staff, and miners' houses, where they were bathed in a tin bath by their wives in front of the fire. As a child, I was only vaguely aware that there were other sorts of existences like that. I had no idea of the kind of grinding poverty and appalling conditions of the 1930s.

A number of books of his photographs had already been published by the time I came along and he would go through them with me and tell me about the pictures. He clearly had a great eye for position and design, for the shape of a picture, and was enormously patient in his work. He had to get the conditions absolutely right. We have a picture by Piper of a cleft in the Yorkshire moors called Gordale Scar. At the top of the Scar is a small tree. Uncle Bill went to photograph this tree. He went there on one of those days when the sun was in and out. When the sun was shining, the tree appeared very clearly, but when it went behind a cloud, it was more obscure. There were also climbers ascending the cliff.

It took all day until the moment came when there were no climbers and the sun was shining.

He trained in Vienna with various of the older photographers, then worked at a studio in Paris for three years and managed a studio back in Vienna, Atelier Kolliner. He came to London in 1934. He was very quiet, modest and shy. Later, there was a television programme about certain great photographers including him and people like Cartier-Bresson. The interviewer turned over the photographs, and Bill talked about them. In one of them, there was a picture of the mill town of Halifax in Yorkshire. There was a cobbled street going down, a factory chimney on one side, a railway, and a great big building. The interviewer said, "It's an enormously composed photograph." Bill replied, "Yes. I didn't change anything. It was like that." But he had seen it. Then there was another one shot in Limehouse, of gas lamps and a wall, and a narrow street, and a policeman standing under the gas lamp. And he said, "I was watching that scene, and suddenly the policeman came and stood under the lamp and looked at the camera. It was just right. It made the picture."

Uncle Bill would often come and stay with us too. He got on very well with my father. They were different personalities, but brothers are often like that. I was not aware that he was distinguished when I was growing up. I went through a stage when I was at university and had a camera, and he would say to me, "Look, take a photograph from here, because you've got the foreground and the background…" He gave quite a few pointers.

He did not have a family. He was married to someone called Eva Szerena von Zelenei Szikra Boros, who was Hungarian, but they divorced around the end of the War. Then he married Marjorie, an Englishwoman, with whom he was extremely happy. They lived in Airlie Gardens and my wife and I would often go and have dinner with them. They exuded happiness. She looked after him, because he was a diabetic and had to have a particular diet. At one point, because of his diabetes, he was going blind, so he was put on to a diet with no animal fats, which meant they ate a great deal of fish. She took a lot of trouble to get the diet absolutely right and saved his eyesight as a result.

He always saw wonderful things. When my grandfather died, the family bought from the executors the things that they wanted, and the rest were sold publicly. My grandfather had a marvellous doorstop, which was a claw with a ball inside it. The ball was loose. My Uncle Bill loved this. "Fantastic, it's a real claw," he enthused. He bought a lot of statues and things from my grandfather's garden, some of which we have at our own home in Suffolk.

He took photographs for *Lilliput* and *Harper's Bazaar*. He did a whole series on the English at home and also photographed Impressionist artists of the time, and he would tell me of the experiences he had. *Harper's* asked him to photograph Picasso. Picasso was extremely shy and diffident about being photographed or even meeting outsiders. So Uncle Bill had to devise a way of photographing him. He hung around

Bill Brandt, 1904–1983.

outside Picasso's house in the South of France, until eventually the artist asked him what he was doing there. Uncle Bill admired the woman living with Picasso, who was extremely attractive. So he said, "Would you allow me to photograph her?" And Picasso said, "Yes, all right." So he set the girl up and photographed her from a number of different angles. And Picasso, in the background, began to insinuate himself into the shots, because he was rather jealous. He made faces and fooled about, and finally, Bill got the opportunity: "Why don't I photograph you?" Picasso assented. That is how he did it.

He was also asked by *Harper's Bazaar* to go down and photograph J. Paul Getty and Sutton Place. He was with a group of journalists who went down together, with Getty. They stopped somewhere on the way down to Guildford, in a pub, and somehow the journalists manoeuvred the thing so that Getty did not pay their bill. Then they produced a headline saying, "Getty doesn't even pay the bill." Uncle Bill told me it was an absolute monstrous exploitation to put Getty in that position.

Uncle Bill did not like giving interviews. He would never push himself forward. He would, however, find clever ways of inserting himself, inoffensively, into someone's life, so that he could photograph them. He came and photographed us all at the bank once. But it was a formal kind of picture.

Uncle Rudolf
The third brother, Uncle Rudolf, known as Rolf, was born in Hamburg in 1906 and educated there. In line with family tradition, he began a commercial apprenticeship with Albert Boesenberg in 1925, but then changed direction. He moved to Berlin to study art and theatre history the following year. He attended the Kalbeck Theatre School in Vienna from 1927 to 1928 and also took lessons with an elocutionist called Müller in Berlin. He was given a position in the Youth Comedy department at Friedrichs Theatre, Dessau, in autumn 1929, where he remained until 1931. After that he acted with the Emelka Film Association in Munich and Berlin and at the Münchener Kammerspiele, and was a

member of the Schiller Theatre Ensemble in Berlin. He went to London in autumn 1933 and entered the Royal Academy of Dramatic Arts.

He worked at London theatres and television until 1938, then joined the Fire Service in London when the War broke out and worked there for its duration. Afterwards he did graphical work and illustrations for various publishers and magazines, exhibition murals and other artistic projects. In 1949 he started teaching and was visiting lecturer at the Borough Polytechnic, then joined the London College of Printing the following year and was appointed senior lecturer almost ten years later. He had exhibitions of his work at the Arts Council, Artists International Association, Institute of Contemporary Art, London Group, Paris Gallery (London) and Galleria Pater, Milan, from 1954 to 1969. The pictures he painted were quite interesting and I think for a while quite popular.

He had three children; I am still in touch with a daughter. But he and my father became estranged early on over political differences, and his son Nicholas somehow continued that feud even after my father's death. Uncle Rudolf died on 30 January 1986. My brother Denis and I, because of this acrimony, were not invited to the funeral, but we went anyway. He was our uncle, after all. And anyway, the enmity did not make sense. Liza and I had once visited Rolf, as he was known, and we had a wonderful, hilarious time.

Uncle Augustus
My father's youngest brother was Augustus. He was born in 1911, so he was nine years younger than my father. He had attended the Heinrich-Hertz-Realgymnasium in Hamburg, and then in 1928 the Zugerberg Commercial School at Zug in Switzerland. He apprenticed in his father's business L. W. Brandt & Co. in Hamburg from 1929 to 1931, then completed his training at the Business Training Corporation in London, entering Wm. Brandt's Sons & Co. as an employee in 1932. In 1934 he moved to become an employee at Pargola Ltd., a firm of rubber dealers associated with the Brandt firm.

Between 1936 and 1937 he travelled extensively in South Africa, East Africa, India, Burma, the Malay Peninsula, the Dutch East Indies, Australia, New Zealand, the Philippines, Hong Kong, China and Japan, returning to Europe via Canada and the USA. In 1938 he took up permanent residence in Sydney, Australia. At the outbreak of the Second World War he enlisted in the Royal Australian Air Force. After training in Australia, Canada and Britain, he passed out as a Sergeant Observer in a bomber squadron. Returning from night operations over the Ruhr district of Germany during the night of the 6th/7th April 1942, his Stirling bomber crashed in the North Sea. His body was the only one of the crew to be recovered, having been washed ashore on the coast of Schleswig-Holstein in June 1942. He was buried by the Germans in a collective grave as "unknown enemy airman". After the occupation of Germany by the Allies, the grave was opened by the Inter-Allied War Graves Commission and his body was identified and re-interred in the British Military Cemetery at Kiel, where he is at rest in Grave 15, Row H, Plot 2.

Augustus was my godfather as well as my uncle. My father was clearly very fond of him, as one would be of one's youngest brother. I well remember the moment when he came into my bedroom early in the morning, and said, "Uncle Gugu's been killed." It was my first real encounter with death. I remember my father standing there in his dark suit, about to go to the office; it was probably half past seven in the morning and they had received the news. Then he went off to London. I was eleven years old and did not really grasp it. Uncle Augustus was someone whom we saw every year or so, who suddenly was no longer there.

Death was something my father and I did not talk about. He was rather like me with emotional subjects: I do not necessarily go to anybody with them. I tend to work them out for myself. There is always a tendency to brush them under the carpet of course, but I think they get dealt with sooner or later.

Religion was never very much part of my life either, and certainly not in my childhood, apart from what developed in myself. I did go to church when I went to prep school and we had chapel every day and on Sundays. It was not anything to do with my parents. My mother was spiritual rather than religious.

I do have religious beliefs now, but they are not terribly well articulated. I am not completely sure whether there is anything after death. In many ways I ask myself, is religion something thought up by man to provide him with an answer to all the unanswered questions? Right from time immemorial: take the simple peasant who cannot understand why his crops are destroyed by rain, and the only thing he can do is to appeal to something bigger. Even today, I think man is inclined to believe that his intelligence is so important that it cannot just last a lifetime: he cannot actually admit that. That is one side of it, and religion provides the answer to all that. But whether there is a life hereafter, and whether one's spirit goes on or not, I do not know.

Having said this, when my mother died, she had been in the house alone down in Essex and we went there from London the moment we heard the news. From there, my wife and I went to our home in Suffolk, and I remember having this extraordinary feeling of my mother sort of soaring overhead. She was still there. Then it faded. At her funeral, we were talking about parents and the past and the future with a friend of ours who lived in the village, and they said, "Well, they live on through you."

This is true. We have a lot of the things they collected around us. When my father died, his watercolour collection was inherited jointly by my brother and me. My brother was less interested in it, so I took it over from him and my wife and I continued to nurture and update it. People have often visited and said, "Oh yes, I remember going to your parents and looking at your father's watercolour collection, and I had a very nice lunch with your mother." People doing research, studying a particular artist, come from America and visit for the day. They look at some of our pictures, have lunch, and we talk about things one would not normally talk about at all, because we are otherwise not part of their world. That really stems from my father, so it is continuing the work he did. There are a lot of links.

There are also a lot of lessons that my mother gave me which I continue to remember. One of the things she said was, "You know, if you want something badly enough, and you're determined enough to get it, you will succeed."

Schooldays

Our family used to go on holiday to a village in Cornwall called Trebetherick. When the Second World War broke out, my parents did not want us to stay in London. In theory, my mother could have taken us away to America, but she was quite clear that she was the wife of an Englishman and we would stay in England. There was no question about it.

So they approached the people in Cornwall whose house we had taken for a holiday the previous summer and we moved there in early September 1939. It was called Trefelix and was owned by Sir John and Lady Walsham, who had returned from Shanghai ten years before and built it. The place was filled with Chinese artefacts and memorabilia: beautiful carpets, vases, and dragons in a sunken garden with Chinese tiles in among the borders.

The village of Trebetherick is also where John Betjeman spent his holidays. I am fond of him because of the way he writes about the village's, St. Enodoc's Church and its bellringers and about Cornwall generally. I also like Victorian railways and other things he was interested in. Many of the books in the bookshelves of Trefelix had the name 'Biddy Walsham' inscribed in them – presumably a daughter of the family – and Biddy Walsham is a subject of Betjeman's writings, so he obviously knew them.

We stayed there for about two years while the War raged. We saw Plymouth burning forty miles away. I went to a school which had been evacuated from the Home Counties somewhere, which was run by Arthur Ransome's brother. He used to sit on the table and swing his legs. It was a mile from the house and if I missed the bus, I could walk, which seemed quite grown up at the time. I was very much an outsider at school, because I was a day boy and the others were all boarding. When they got down to their recreation, I went home. We called the school Ransomes, but I think it was actually called West Hill. By a strange coincidence, Martin Mays-Smith, to whom I will later refer, was there too, although I did not know him at the time. Ransome taught me Latin there. Later I studied Classics until I left Eton. I was not a classical scholar in the true sense, but I enjoyed it and was good at it, precisely because he gave me such a good grounding. And I was only with him for two terms.

The rest of my preparatory schooling happened at St Ronan's in Kent. Its headmaster was the one who first told me about sex. He did it extremely well and made it very much part of love and marriage, and not in any way offensive. I would have been twelve. He took each of us in quietly and spent an hour with us in his study. He also prepared us for Confirmation, so we had a period in our lives, if we were confirmed, in our last year at the school, when we had quite a lot of dealings of a relatively personal nature with him. I think he told my parents that he had talked to me, and therefore they did not need to go over the subject with me. It was much easier for someone like him to do that. He was a bachelor and extremely good with the boys.

I went to Eton in Michaelmas 1944, aged 13. Going there had always been part of the programme. My mother being American and my father having been brought up abroad, neither of them knew the British educational scene particularly well. All my mother knew was that Eton was the best school she had ever heard of, and that was where her son was going. My opinion was not asked, nor did it occur to me to resist in any way.

It was the end of the War, so things were fairly austere – which they were in English boarding schools anyway. Things have changed since. Back then it was unheated and there were a lot of shortages.

It was much larger than any school I had been to before, but divided into houses of forty boys, so you lived in a small community. The biggest class I was in had about 25 boys in it, but most were around 15.

It was not intimidating, except for the fact that I was a very small person in a large school, with a lot of people who were a great deal older. The difference between 13 and 18 is substantial. And these were boys who, at age 18, were going to leave and go off to the war that was ongoing. But I got used to that disparity after about the first term and made friends easily, some of whom have remained close.

One man I mentioned previously was Martin Mays-Smith. He was a new boy with me at Eton, and in the same house. We rowed together. He did his National Service in the Army, not the Navy like me. We shared rooms afterwards when we got to Cambridge. After that we both worked in the City, he in the Bank of England and I at William Brandt's; he eventually joined us there in about 1968. When I was younger, I used to go and have dinner with his father Robin, who would give general advice about life. He was extremely good with young men, as, actually, are his two sons. They have a way of talking easily with young people on quite intimate subjects.

Martin was intelligent and we had many shared interests, first among which was rowing. Then there was the fact that, in each house at Eton, there are only about five new boys a year, so we were a small group.

Peter, Denis and Walter.

He was not my main friend at Eton though. There was someone else called David Barlow, whom I also knew later at Cambridge. There was another man there too who later joined us at the firm: William Wilkinson. He was the son of my housemaster, Dennis Wilkinson, whom I shall mention presently. He also went on to Trinity in Cambridge, where he became a good friend. Martin Mays-Smith knew him at Eton, and when Martin and I shared rooms at Cambridge, William came and saw us quite a lot. That is how I got to know him.

The school qualification in those days was called the School Certificate. I do not think I got any distinctions, but I got a reasonable number of credits. I did not go on to do A-levels, because my housemaster Dennis Wilkinson decided I was busy enough elsewhere and did not need to do them. He had an ulterior motive. I was the senior oarsman in his house during my last year and I ran all the rowing. Wilkinson was keen that we should do well in the rowing, so he opted me out of A-levels under the pretext that I looked too tired.

This did not affect my future at all. Exams were much less important then than now. You did not necessarily get into Cambridge solely on your A-levels. In my case, the admissions tutor at Trinity, Walter Hamilton, had been an Eton master and was a very good friend of Dennis Wilkinson. A phone call and a recommendation from Wilkinson was enough.

Dennis Wilkinson was probably the most important influence over my life at Eton, and perhaps over my life subsequently. He supported his boys to the hilt, whatever they did. He was also my classical tutor. He had created a specialist class called Classics General, which was a grade down from the boys who did Classics proper, most of whom were in the sixth form and very clever. Dennis had suggested that there were a group of boys who would benefit from doing Classics, but not at quite such a high level as the boys at the top of the school. I was one of them. I saw a great deal of him in my last two years at school.

The essence of the Classical education that he provided was reading a lot of Greek, Latin and English literature, which he encouraged us in.

He was also good at teaching us to write English. There are all sorts of little rules and philosophies of life which I have drawn from him. And there was another aspect of what he gave us, which was what you might call character.

When it came to Cambridge, he was quite clear which College I would go to. It was entirely his influence and decision really, and I have never regretted it. It was one of the best things I ever did. He and I also discussed what I was going to read there. I thought it would be modern languages, because I was interested in them. But he said, "Why do you want to do that?" I said, "Well, because I think it's a good way of learning languages." "Don't be silly," he replied. "Go and learn something useful and practical, and if you want to learn languages, go abroad during the long vacations." So that is exactly what I did. I went abroad almost every holiday – Christmas, Easter and the long summer break. And at Cambridge I read Economics and Law.

We had learned French at school, and a certain amount of German. I went and practised my French by living in Paris, and I learned Italian, which I also did at school, but fairly cursorily, by going to Florence for the whole of the summer vacation.

In Paris I lived in a large house owned by a woman who had a number of people staying there as paying guests. We all ate at a communal table. Everyone was friendly and talked to me, which was the object of the exercise. I did have lessons too: someone came a few times a week and spoke to me for an hour or two. Apart from that, I went to museums and talked to people I met.

In Florence, I stayed with a marvellous lady called the Marquesa Patrizi and went to Florence University for two months to study Italian and the development of Italian Art. This Marquesa had a large flat and two or three paying guests like me. We sat at her dining room table for meals and she would talk to us and help us learn Italian. She also sent us on various excursions. She said, "If you're interested in pictures, go to such-and-such a house on such-and-such a street and ring the doorbell." A guardian would appear and take us into a cloister, where there would be some marvellous Italian picture which nobody saw unless they knew about it.

The Navy

My mother, very shortly after my birth, had my horoscope done, and one of the things it said was that I would always gain pleasure and success from things connected with water. This turned out to be true. I loved the sea. I rowed successfully at Eton. I joined the Navy for my National Service and became a naval officer. Then I rowed successfully at Cambridge and I even rowed for Britain at the Olympics. I am still connected with my College boat club; I coached them in the summer for decades. And I was a Board Member of the National Rivers Authority. So water has been a constant theme of pleasure and success throughout my life.

I left Eton in 1949 and went straight into the Royal Navy around October. I was absolutely determined to go there. I had two naval cousins, the Ashmores. They had become senior officers by 1949 and they said I should join the Royal Naval Volunteer Reserve as a junior rating, which I did. That meant during the last two holidays of my time at Eton, I served on a Naval vessel once for three weeks, then later for a fortnight. I am short-sighted and therefore could not be what they call a seaman, so I went into the paymaster branch. I spent something like six months on a ship called HMS *Ceres*, in the middle of Yorkshire (many shore establishments are known as ships), where we were trained as paymasters. During that time I also went before what is called the Admiralty Selection Board and was chosen to be trained as an officer. By about May or June 1950, I was a midshipman. I learned from the Ashmores that if you wanted anything in the Navy, you wrote immediately to your captain or to the First Lords of the Admiralty and asked to do it. I did this and said I wished to be sent abroad, the alternative being service in Londonderry, which I dreaded.

I was sent to Malta and spent a year there. I went out on a troop ship and arrived there in the middle of July. It was the hottest place I had ever been in my life, but very attractive, surrounded by the wonderful

85

Mediterranean. I was sent to an air station to learn air stores, which are a rather particular branch of the Navy, then I went to a submarine depot ship called HMS *Forth*, where I worked with Captain Tony Myers. It was said you either got on with him, or you left his ship immediately. My response was the former. He was a dynamo of a man with phenomenal energy. He had a VC, DSO and Bar, all for service in submarines during the War. He used to sweep aside all sorts of red tape and bureaucracy. To receive his VC, he was summoned to the Palace, as is customary. But he said, "I'm bringing my crew." They refused. "Then I'm not coming." After much debate, the Palace relented and he arrived with a 70-man crew to receive his VC from the King.

He would quite often step in on behalf of a rating – in a disciplinary matter, for instance, if he thought it was not entirely the rating's fault and perhaps an officer had been partly negligent and caused the trouble. He would get hold of me and say, "I want you to write to the C-in-C immediately." I would sit down and write, he would sign it and he would say, "Right, take that to the C-in-C at once."

I did a lot of jobs like that. Then there came a time in about February or March 1951 when for six weeks I became his personal secretary, doing everything. It was a tremendous experience. Things were formal in the Navy, but he was an informal being. I would call him "Sir", but he would call me Peter. Occasionally, if I did something wrong, he blew up.

Someone from my old prep school whom I met in Portsmouth before going to the Mediterranean said, "If you're going to Malta, buy yourself a motorcycle when you get there." So I did. You could buy one for 15 pounds in those days. I managed to take it quite often on our cruises. I had the motorcycle in the tank landing ship. In Algiers I went shopping with Captain Myers riding pillion. He went on to become a Rear-Admiral. I stayed in touch with him and he came and made the speech at our wedding at two days' notice, since the family friend who was going to do it had fallen ill.

National Service matured me. I saw a lot of the world and did a serious job in which things mattered and people depended on what you did. In HMS *Forth*, there were about 15 midshipmen, and we all lived together in the same mess. Those midshipmen, the same age as I, handled the boats which took sailors from ship to shore and back. Once, there had been a bad storm and the ship was lying quite a way off the shore. There were a lot of men who had been effectively trapped in the little port. One midshipman came to fetch them in a boat called a cutter, which took about 100 passengers. He was in charge and had two sailors to help him. He went over the bar and it was very rough – quite a daunting experience for such a young man. He said to me afterwards he had to pay close attention, otherwise the boat could have been turned over. That is what the Navy does: it gives you a lot of responsibility at a young age.

National Service has its benefits. The difficulty for young men and women at the moment is that they leave school at 18 and have to decide what they are going to do next. But how, at that age, do you actually know what you want to do? It takes a few years to find out. Life for me was, in that sense, very much easier. I knew exactly what I was going to do. I wanted to go into the Navy, I knew I was going to do National Service, and that was going to be eighteen months or two years. It was a valuable stepping-stone to the rest of my life. And it provides you with very good discipline, because all the armed services are well-disciplined.

Cambridge

Cambridge was quite different to what it is today. There were virtually no women. There were two women's colleges, I think: Girton and Newnham. Apart from that, it was an all-male society. Girls arrived on two great occasions in the year for the balls, one at the end of the Lent Term, the other at the end of the Summer Term. The whole place was suddenly alive with all sorts of pretty people in pretty dresses. It made a very pleasant change. But on the whole, I did not particularly miss women being around.

WM. BRANDT'S SONS & CO.

Blade of an oar (scull) inscribed with Peter's part in the Olympic Games of 1952.

I rowed for my College and I was secretary and later captain of its boat club. In my first year at Cambridge I rowed at the Olympic Games in Helsinki in double sculls. But we did not do very well.

Looking back, I do value the Economics I studied, but I found it fairly dry and boring and I changed to Law for my last two years, which I enjoyed enormously. I enjoyed the arguments and the logical development of a case, and I was really quite sorry I had not done Law the whole time.

My studies were very valuable for my subsequent work in the City. To have just a feeling for the law is extremely worthwhile – the basic bones of it. I have sometimes thought it might have been nice to have done something like English Literature, because one of the advantages of a university education is that it can provide an opportunity to study a subject in depth – a subject you may never get the time or opportunity to study again.

The majority of my closest friends were from Cambridge. There was Martin Mays-Smith, whom I have mentioned before, who, although he happens to have been an Etonian, was really a Cambridge acquaintance. The same goes for William Wilkinson, the son of my housemaster. He got a scholarship to Cambridge and was a scholar at Eton. After Cambridge he lived a rather different life. He went and worked for Borax and lived in Turkey for a while. Much later, he came to William Brandt's for about three years, then went to Lonrho. He ended up with Kleinworts, and from Kleinworts he went on to become Chairman of the what was then called the Nature Conservancy Council.

THE STORY OF A FAMILY TRADING COMPANY

Peter with his mother and father aboard the Queen Mary on their way to his brother's wedding via New York, 1964.

Someone called Ray Lister was also at Trinity with me, and he became a partner of Cazenove. We used to see him from time to time. I knew many such people. David Coleridge and I were also at school together. He was an extremely nice man and I had always regarded him as an able person, so it was no surprise when he later became Chairman of Lloyd's of London.

Aside from friends at Cambridge, another influential person for me was a Director of Studies called Bill Wade. He was a law lecturer and also happened to be treasurer of Trinity Boat Club, so I had a dual relationship with him. He went on being an acquaintance, because in 1963 I was invited to go back and coach the Trinity crew for the summer races, which I then continued to do right up to 1998. Bill Wade became Master of Caius and was a great supporter of its boat club, and we competed from time to time, so we used to see each other on the towpath.

Much later, I was the secretary of a dining club and I got him to come and talk there about proportional representation and constitutional reform.

I also knew Penelope Gilliatt at Cambridge, although I had met her long before. Her parents, the Conners, were great friends of my parents. As a child, I was taken off to stay for weekends with the Conners, and Penelope was there. Cyril Conner seemed to be a slightly puritanical, correct man, whereas Mary, his wife, was giggling good fun. They eventually divorced. We stayed with them in a perfectly ordinary little house in Studland, near Bournemouth, then later up in Northumberland, which must have been Easter 1938.

At that stage, Penelope was just a girl I played with, the way you do at the age of six or seven. It was much later, when I was leaving Eton and joining the Navy, that I got to know her better. She was very appealing, a lot of fun, and clever. She did quite a lot of good for me and got me interested in music. She became a great girlfriend while I was in the Navy, but I was in Malta and she was in England and I do not think we even necessarily wrote, except the occasional postcard. Then, when I went to Cambridge, she became my girlfriend proper and used to come

Liza Brandt.

Peter Brandt.

up if I was in a rowing event. She went with me to Henley and came to the May Ball in my first year.

She had a rough sort of life later on, but we had a lot of fun together and I would not have predicted that things would go the way they did for her. I think my parents saw it though. They were extremely worried that I was going to marry her, which I did consider, as you would aged twenty with an attractive girl on your arm with whom you get on extremely well. It remained platonic though. It was the 1950s, after all.

She was my only real girlfriend until the relationship cooled, as relationships often do at that sort of age. Then for a while there was nobody in particular, until I left Cambridge, then I was great friends with the sister of a man called James Stirling, a friend of mine from Cambridge. I walked out with her for a year or two, before I went and worked in Hamburg and she went her own way.

Liza

Elisabeth ten Bos, who I would marry, came later. I was living in a flat in London, up on Marylebone Road. She and I had met at a cocktail party given by William Wilkinson, very shortly after I returned from my trip around the world, which I will describe later. Liza was doing temporary secretarial work in London. She was very attractive and had an enormous amount of practical common sense. Those were her two principal characteristics. I know now that if I had consulted her an awful lot more along the way, I would have made fewer mistakes than I actually made. She was an enormous help to me during my difficulties with my father at William Brandt's. She was great fun, and among other things took me parachuting. In spite of this rather reckless approach to life, we had a long and very happy marriage until she died in May 2018.

Liza's parents were Dutch. But she and her siblings were all born in England (except Kate, the youngest, who was born in Scotland in 1942). My father-in-law had seen what had happened during the First World War and he wanted his children to have British passports. Although

Liza sharing Peter's life-long passion for steam.

Peter and his steam car.

they lived in Holland and Belgium, two weeks before confinement, my mother-in-law would arrive in London, have the baby, register it as British by birth, get the passport and go back home.

When the Second World War did finally come, they were living in Brussels. It must have been around May 1940 when my father-in-law said to his family, "We must go." They put all the luggage they could fit into a little car, locked the front door of their house and drove off to the channel ports to go to England. They found all the channel ports blocked, so they made their way down and across to Bordeaux. The whole journey took them about six weeks. My wife remembered it vividly. She was five years old. They slept in churches, they slept in ditches, they saw guns firing. They were part of that great big train of refugees streaming across France.

When they finally got to Bordeaux, they went to the British authorities and said, "We wish to go to England." The British replied, "We're extremely sorry, there are only two ships left, and they must be reserved for British subjects." "Fine," said my mother-in-law, "here are your British subjects." My wife, aged five, her younger brother aged three and a half, and a little girl of nine months. "Here are their passports. Take them to England." And the British authorities said, "Well, they can't travel without their mother of course, so you, Mrs ten Bos, may come." She was a forceful woman. She said, "I am absolutely not travelling without my husband." So they all came on the ship, which was the last one to get through, as the final one after it was sunk by a torpedo.

My father-in-law was a businessman on the Continent. He represented major British firms including Hawker-Siddeley, Vosper Thorneycroft, Westland Helicopters and various other companies, selling their equipment, principally, to the Dutch armed services. So when they arrived as refugees, and with his profile, they were suspected as being infiltrators. The mother and girls were moved into a cinema, where they lived for a few days, and my father-in-law was placed in Wormwood Scrubs jail while they screened him to see whose side he was actually on. But he had always had extremely good contacts in England. He was a member of Whites and had done a great deal for the country. Quite soon he was cleared.

He joined the Dutch Fleet Air Arm. He had had his own aircraft before the War in which he used to fly his pregnant wife across to have their babies. He was stationed in Scotland and lived there until about 1959 or '60. After that, he went back and picked up the threads of his previous business. My mother-in-law carried on living in Scotland, but by the time I first met Liza, they had rented a house in Chester Square, London.

Liza and her sisters had been educated in England at a school called Birklands, near St. Albans in Hertfordshire. We saw each other a lot in the summer of 1959, then in October that year she went to America for two years. But she came back from time to time, and when she did, we saw each other. On one of her trips back to England in 1960 I was about to go South America and I said to her, "Look, I'm going to be in South America in August or September, why don't we meet in Mexico for a holiday?" I knew that an attractive girl in New York would be surrounded by admirers and the only chance of actually getting her on her own was to do something like that. To my pleasant surprise, she said, "Yes, good idea."

It was quite unusual, if you were not married, to go on holiday together. But we behaved very correctly. We spent a bit of time in Mexico City, then went down to Acapulco for about a week, and there we became engaged. When we were together, the feeling was mutual. Who proposed to whom is a question that nobody can answer. I had always assumed I would marry her and I had always wanted children too. It was part of my make-up.

My family were delighted with Liza. I had taken her to Henley Royal Regatta one Saturday, then we drove home and arrived at my parents' house during the night and went to bed. She had not met my parents before. She got down to breakfast before I did, and my mother came rushing upstairs and said, "Absolutely marvellous."

The wedding took place in the Church of St. Bartholomew-the-Great in Smithfield, which is a lovely Norman church, London's oldest surviving one. We had the reception walking distance away at the Butchers' Hall – not because of the connections which I had by then established with the meat trade, but because of friends of Liza's. There were two or three hundred people there.

We were married in May, and we moved out of my one-bedroom flat on Marylebone Road in December. We had exchanged contracts on a house in Holland Park just before we were married, then we completed just after. In fact, the moment we were engaged, Liza stopped working and devoted herself to finding that house, which took three or four months. She rang up the agents day after day, saying, "Elisabeth ten Bos here, what have you got?"

Our daughter, Katharine, was born on our first wedding anniversary, by three-quarters of an hour. I was present at the birth – almost. I only missed it because the doctor had said, "Well, that's it for the night. You can go home." I got all the way home and had just got into bed when the telephone rang. "You'd better come back." She was born five minutes before I arrived.

While Liza was still in hospital, I was sitting in our kitchen with our daily, who herself had had children. She said, "Mr Brandt, nothing will ever be the same again." But I do not think that fatherhood changed me as such. It was more part of the general development of one's life. I was reasonably involved with our daughter's babyhood. There would be times when I sorted her out in the night and changed her nappy when Liza was asleep. I was ham-handed, but I managed. We had the daily, and we had what in those days was called a 'mother's help', who was a nanny. This we had until the last child went away to school.

Katharine was born in May 1963; Edward in October 1964, and Nicholas in March 1968. I was more involved with the boys later and Liza remained closely involved with Katharine. They each started at a little nursery school three doors away; Katharine, when she was about 14, went to New Hall, near Chelmsford, which was an excellent convent school. Edward went to St. Ronan's prep, where I had been. He also went to a school in Cambridge, then he went first of all to King's School in Bruton, then to Bradfield for his A-levels. Nicholas went to St. Ronan's, then Eton.

In 1970, we bought a 14th-century Suffolk farmhouse called Spout Farm and moved there permanently in 1978. It is in a very pretty situation. It has low ceilings and lots of beams. Below the house is a large pond. We used to keep two horses and my wife and I would ride at weekends, which is good exercise. We did quite a lot of conversion work – moving the drive and things like that. But first we lived in it for about four or five years, then decided what we wanted to change round. We made a lot of friends in the area and we would invite our London friends down for the weekend, but not as much as we wanted to.

William Brandt's of London

It was always quite clear that my father wanted me to go to William Brandt's. I myself looked forward to it. I was interested in the world and in languages, and there was no better place to work internationally than somewhere like William Brandt's, because we traded with the world.

I joined in September 1954. Its offices were at 36 Fenchurch Street. It was a lovely, old-fashioned, family style merchant bank. It had a great

WM. BRANDT'S SONS & CO.

Blank Cheque

big mahogany counter. Everybody sat at desks in rows, with green lamp shades. There was a uniformed porter with a William Brandt's emblem on his buttons, a mahogany staircase, a mahogany panelled first floor, and first floor partners' rooms.

36, Fenchurch Street, London, E.C.3.

I began in what was called the Documentary Credit Division, which deals with payments for imports and exports. It was methodical, clerical work. I handled Letters of Credit, which are documents sent out by a bank, which say that if you do certain things like delivering certain quantities of goods, at a certain price, on a certain ship, then we will pay you. And that is the current way in which trade is financed, except between customers who know each other extremely well and trust each other to perform.

I did that for about three months. It was regarded as very important. It was the nub of the bank's business at the time and the work stood me in very good stead. After that, I went round to the various other departments, including Book-keeping and Cash, and to the Stock Exchange. I enjoyed some of it, but other aspects were naturally very tedious. People do not do those things now. I was a clerical trainee for two years and worked in each department for three or four months.

The other employees treated me with the kind of deferential respect you would expect in a family business. The partners were all called Brandt, and I was called "Mr Peter". But at that stage, I was not yet involved in discussions about the way the bank was run.

Everything there was done by hand. The staff were extremely loyal and very meticulous and conscientious in what they did. At a more senior level – and this was in the City as a whole – if you wanted to talk to another merchant bank with a proposition, you did not do it all on the telephone. You rang them up and said, "I have something I'd like to come and see you about. May I come over?" And you would go and see them. They would do the same with us. You put on your hat (if you wore one) and you went round to Kleinworts, Barings or the others. We had dealings with all the members of the Accepting Houses Committee, which was the core of merchant banking. The merchant banks were also members of a dining club called the Society of Merchants Trading to the Continent, which is what we all did. William Brandt's, Hambros, Kleinwort, Schroders and the rest of them. These people ran the City.

The Great-Uncles at the Bank

After my great-grandfather Augustus Ferdinand retired and went back to Hamburg in 1880 due to ill-health, he made his three sons partners.

The eldest was Augustus Philip, the first of the great-uncles with whom we used to spend Christmas. He had started at Wm. Brandt's Sons & Co. in London as a young man, then his early apprenticeships had taken him to America, then back to Hamburg, then to France, and finally back to the Brandt firm in London, where he was made a partner in 1895.

A great deal of the rapid development in the United States at the start of the twentieth century was being financed by London banks, and Brandt's ended up doing a lot of trading finance for the Americans. Great-Uncle Augustus had married an American lady, Jean Champion Garmany. Later there was an opportunity for Brandt's to establish a bank in New York, because it was easy to get a licence. Schroders did

Augustus Philip Brandt, 1871–1952.   Mrs Augustus P. Brandt (née Jean Champion Garmany), 1900–1973.

it and established Schroder Banking, which became a huge success. We could have done the same, because the clientele and the opportunity were there. My father thought that Great-Uncle Augustus could not be bothered to go to America to do it, despite his American connections and being very involved in our American business. This was the period in history in which America rapidly overtook other nations industrially and the need for finance was huge. Later, when our bank got taken over and ultimately closed, my father and I inevitably looked back rather ruefully on this missed opportunity.

In 1952 Augustus Philip decided to withdraw his capital from the firm. Montague Norman, Governor of the Bank of England, when informed of this, believing that losing such a significant proportion of its total capital would cause irreparable damage to the bank, tried very hard to persuade him to change his mind, but to no avail.

The second of Augustus Ferdinand's sons, Great-Uncle Henry, dealt with South America and the Continent. Like his older brother, he had travelled in his early career, but in his case to Lausanne, Hamburg and Buenos Aires, whence he also toured the Falkland Islands, Chile and Paraguay in 1894. After that he returned to London and became a partner at Wm. Brandt's Sons & Co., also in 1895. But banking was not everything he did. In later life he bred prize-winning bulls at his Capenor estate, pedigree descendants of which are still today farmed and sold as beef. He had horses in the Grand National. One was called Columbus. I bet on him and didn't win any money. It came fourth. But I remember the horse. His trainer was a man called James. James once said to Great-Uncle Henry, "If you knew what went on in the changing rooms, you would give up." Everything was fixed.

Great-Uncle Henry was a shrewd man. In Bremen, in the early 1930s, during the Crash, he was having lunch with a friend and talking about the Bremen firms, and he said, "By the way, that firm over there," pointing to a new building, "what's its name?" His companion told him the name of the firm. Great-Uncle Henry said, "Oh really? I've heard of them and I was going to call on them. But if they spent so much money

Henry Bernhard Brandt, 1872–1958. Portrait by Sir Oswald Birley, 1951.

on a building, I think I'll cross them off my list." They later went bust. He somehow knew. They were a merchant firm: what did they want a huge building for? A merchant firm needs to be liquid, because they have to pay for goods all the time.

There are probably a great many he would cross off his list nowadays. That is also because the other principle he held to and which my father used to instil in us – although we did not really believe him at the time – was: "Never lend to governments, because governments have no morals and they do not mind defaulting." It does not affect them. If you now look around the world, there is massive Third World debt which the big international banks are saddled with. If they had followed that rule, they would not have the troubles they have today. Governments do not mind defaulting. A politician is only there for five years.

Having said that, my peers and I later persuaded my father that this was an outdated view and we did end up lending to governments a bit. We did not actually lose anything, either. They were mainly South

American governments. We lent to South American entities, which had South American government guarantees – Central Bank guarantees.

Great-Uncle Rudolf, the third of the brothers, apprenticed in Hamburg like his brothers, went to work at Wm. Brandt's Sons & Co., and then from 1896–97 he travelled throughout South America, after which he returned to London and became a partner in the firm on 1 January 1899.

He joined the Ministry of Ammunition in 1914 to form the Concentrated Ammonium Section in the High Explosives Department in London. He stayed there until 1916, in which year he joined the Officers Training Corps, being stationed near Chelmsford in Essex, until the end of the War. He accompanied his nephew William on a trip to Canada, in 1920. As well as his work at Brandt's, he was a director of London Assurance from 1912 to 1943. During World War II, while the junior partners of Brandt's were away on War Service, he attended the office every day without a break.

Great-Uncle Rudolf thought up a number of new ideas related to the firm. We still had relatives in Russia, Arthur Gutschow and Olga,

Rudolf Ernst Brandt, 1874–1961.

Panoramic View of St Petersburg, by M. V. Dobuzhinsky, 1912.

right up until the Revolution and beyond. Just after the Revolution, two of them living in St. Petersburg were timber agents. It must have been about 1920 when the man and his wife decided they had to leave. They took all the jewellery they had, put it into their fur-lined Russian overcoats, and in the dead of winter, during the night, walked across the ice to Finland and escaped. From Finland they sent a telegram to Great-Uncle Rudi, saying they had been timber agents in St. Petersburg, they would like to set up a timber agency in Finland. Would he please lend them £20,000 to do so? He cabled back that he would not lend them £20,000, but if they came to London, he would give them unlimited credit and offices in which to establish a timber agency in London. Which they did, and out of that grew a company called William Brandt's Timber, which, when I left the bank, was one of the six largest timber agents in the country. Great-Uncle Rudi knew it was a very sensible diversification for William Brandt's, because the timber agency business is not so much about selling timber, it is about financing it.

It is tempting to connect this story of escape and good fortune with Cousin Olga, whose biography was unknown to me as a child but whose details in Amburger's *Familie Brandt* book correspond intriguingly closely with the people who founded William Brandt's Timber.

According to Amburger, a distant cousin, Arthur Gütschow, was born in 1873 and Olga in 1881, both in Petersburg. They had married there in 1908. In his entry about Great-Uncle Rudolf, written in 1937, it says, 'Since 1899 he has lived in London, now at 22 Down Street, where Arthur and Olga Gütschow also settled after fleeing Russia in 1920.' So Cousin Olga of the lorgnette could well be one of the two people who escaped the Revolution across the ice. But we may never know for certain.

Great-Uncle Rudolf never married. He lived in Gower Street and was quite artistic; he collected paintings and works of art. A Bari bronze we still have in the family came from him. We also have a Corot which he had collected; he had six of them at one point and one is now in the National Gallery.

Sojourn in Germany

After training for two years, I went and worked for a year in Germany – firstly to learn German; secondly to learn about German banking systems and see a different side of commercial life. I spent about three months with a German merchant bank, run in Hamburg by a cousin of ours, Heinrich Berenberg Gossler, during which time I also had German lessons. I lived in a German household and spoke only German the whole time I was there.

It was a private bank. They financed trade and had their own customers. They did it in a different way, because the German banking system is different, but the style of the place was very similar – oak panelling and a marvellous old porter who had been in place for fifty years and would always talk about "Herr Baron", because the owner was actually Baron Heinrich Berenberg Gossler. There was a deferential air.

The air was similar in London too, and I think I derided that kind of hierarchy a bit at the time, because I thought it was old-fashioned and we ought to move on. Now I look back on it with a degree of nostalgia. People behaved very decently with one another – despite being quite robust in the cut and thrust of commerce. They were always very polite. Telephone conversations did not have to be recorded. You did not have to write everything down, because you knew that if John Baring – to use a London example – had said yes, then it was yes. You did, of course, confirm things by writing, but that was not the essence of things.

It was a case of iron hands in velvet gloves though, because they were all tough people. These were very successful banks, those that are still there today, and they only got there by being commercially astute. The style of the buildings exuded solidity and years of history, which I think has been lost in some more modern buildings.

After my time at the bank in Hamburg, I worked for a subsidiary of Unilever for two or three months. It was very interesting, because it was an industrial operation, quite different from anything I had seen before.

The contacts I made in Germany remained important for some time, but when I left William Brandt's and went in completely different directions, they were lost and I never revived them.

Germany was really for my personal development, to see a whole range of different activities, some of which I tried to apply when I got back. After the Unilever subsidiary, I worked at the export department of another private family bank in Hamburg. That particular work was extremely valuable and I did translate some of it back into William Brandt's later on.

Back in London

When I first started at Brandt's it was run by five partners: Great-Uncle Henry and Great-Uncle Rudolf whom I have mentioned, Henry's son Willy, Willy's brother Henry, and my father. John, Willy's son, who was therefore my second cousin, became a partner before I did.

Willy was born in 1897 and had had an eventful military career before coming to Brandt's. Educated at Rugby School, he joined the army in 1915 and was sent to the French front with the Sherwood Foresters. He was wounded by a bullet through the foot at the Battle of the Somme in September 1916. His recovery took until early the next year, upon which he returned to his battalion. He was made a Captain that same year, took part in heavy fighting and was awarded the Military Cross.

William Edward Brandt, 1897–1987.

In 1918 he turned down every offer of employment with the Staff or as a training officer for the Americans, remained at the front line, took part in the advance in autumn, and was seriously wounded by a shell at Forêt de Mormal eight days before the Armistice. He lay in hospital at Rouen for four weeks and teetered on the brink of death; only in early December was he able to return to London, where a further operation was required to remove shrapnel. Discharged and sent home, he recovered slowly and was sent to travel in June 1919 to regain his health. He returned from this world tour in summer 1920 and took up employment at Wm. Brandt's Sons & Co. He worked from 1921 to 1922 at the Société d'Importation et de Commission Louis Reinhart in Le Havre, 1922–23 at Ludwig Tillmann in Hamburg, and then in London again after that. He became a partner at Brandt's on 1 January 1927.

Willy's brother Henry was born in 1902 and was therefore too young to go to the Great War. Also educated at Rugby, he spent six months in France in 1920 to learn the language. He then attended Oxford University from 1920 until 1922, studied for six months at the Business Training Corporation in London the same year, then became an employee at Wm. Brandt's Sons & Co. From 1924 to 1925 he worked in Hamburg for H. C. Bock, Hugo Stinnes and Ludwig Tillmann, and in

Henry Augustus Brandt, 1902–1986.

1926 in New York for Bingham & Co. Inc., the financial agent of Wm. Brandt's Sons & Co. He set off on a voyage around the world in 1927 to broaden his knowledge, stopping at various cities in the United States, then joined up with my father and visited Japan, China, Indo-China, the Malay States, Java, Sumatra, Siam, Burma and India. Henry worked at Wm. Brandt's Sons & Co. again from 1928 to 1930 and was made a partner on 1 January 1931.

Beneath these experienced and well-travelled family partners were, quite simply, lots of clerks. There was no middle-management at all. To me, this was very behind the times. I wanted to recruit graduates. I assumed that people with a university education were bound to be better than people who were simply automatons doing their job, and if we were going to lead the bank forward, we needed a range of more educated people with initiative and leadership.

It seemed so obvious. The partners did not adopt the idea with enthusiasm, but they went along with it slowly and we recruited two or three graduates within about two years. My father was more supportive than the other two older men. I do not think the others thought their own positions might in some way be threatened, they just had not really thought about it. It had always been run by members of the family – "the management" – along with people who did what they were told. I think it created a certain amount of arrogance in the partners.

When I joined, Augustus, the oldest of my great-uncles, was 83 and had already taken his money out of the firm, to the fury of Montague Norman at the Bank of England, who said it would wreck the bank. In retrospect, Augustus's withdrawal of funds was another seed of our subsequent demise. Great-Uncle Rudolf was 80 and still there, although very much retiring; he came in occasionally. Henry was 82 and actively involved. He attended the partners' meetings once a week and in a way was quite pushy for new ideas, but at the same time cautious. He always used to say, "We ought to deal with so and so… but be careful." He had not thought it sensible for me to go to Cambridge. He thought I should go straight into the firm and start working, because that is what his own grandson, John Brandt, had done. That was his outlook. He did not see the value of recruiting graduates either.

Of all the partners, I think my father was probably dominant. He did all the foreign business. He spoke German fluently, because he had

The Boardroom at Wm. Brandt's. Standing, John M. Brandt (right); sitting, William Edward Brandt (2nd from left), Henry Augustus Brandt (4th from left), Walter Augustus Brandt (5th from left).

been brought up in Hamburg. That was quite important, so he was quite central and he wanted to thrust ahead and do different things. Yet because it was a partnership, they had to have consensus, and the other two were more conservative, one of them in particular. If they did not agree, nobody could say, "Well, this is the way it's going to be." There was not a chairman. It was quite paralysing. As a result, the bank never modernised until it was too late. There must have been some quite serious strains between the partners of which I was not aware.

John went into the timber side of the business with his uncle, Henry Augustus. He concentrated entirely on that, going to Sweden for about two years to train in timber companies there, after which he returned to London and became a managing director. William Brandt's Timber continued long after his tragic death in a car accident. His funeral was attended by members of the Russian Trade Delegation. He was very much an ally and a very good friend. Despite not going to university, he did see the need to have graduates higher up, to keep up with the times otherwise it was just going to be he and I, and both of us saw that you

John Brandt (bottom right).

could not move into the 21st century like that. We did not realise that things would not last long enough to find out.

One of the graduates we employed was Alastair Thompson, who came from Magdalene College, Cambridge, where I had known him. We gave him time off to become a barrister and he gradually developed into the bank's lawyer and drew up special agreements and so on, although that is not all he did. The other man was Owen Humphreys, who came from Oxford and was with us for about a year, then he moved elsewhere. They started the thing going and we began to recruit others. Some fell by the wayside, others stayed. But gradually, over the following ten years, we recruited a proper layer of middle management.

There were other younger members of the family also working in the bank: my brother Denis and my cousins Nigel and Timothy. Timothy was still a trainee when he died in the Windhoek air disaster in 1968. He had gone out to South Africa to visit his wife's family and they both died on their way home. Nigel worked in the Foreign Exchange department looking after customers, and spent time in Buenos Aires. Denis worked in the Investment department having followed in the family tradition, working in different departments of the bank from 1958 to 1960 before going to Munich to work for Merck Fink, and then New York to work for Clark Dodge and Co, then Goldman Sachs, and finally GH Walker before returning to William Brandt's in 1964.

Denis Brandt.

Nigel Brandt.

Timothy Brandt.

World Tour

The firm sent me away on tour for two years, beginning on 1 June 1957. I went by sea to Rio, then flew in stages down to Uruguay, then Buenos Aires, then crossed the Andes by train. There I met a man who became a very great friend, a Chilean lawyer by the name of Enrique Puga. He had a tremendous sense of humour and we got on terribly well. His father was the Chilean ambassador in Washington at the time.

I worked my way up the west coast of South America, ending in Venezuela, and crossed to Cuba. It was just before Castro; they were fighting in the east and Havana was in the west. I moved to the USA, then went by train all the way up from New Orleans to Chicago, crossed in stages to the East Coast, staying with my mother's sister's family for a few days in Cleveland on the way. They were very nice and it was all quite fun and jolly. There was I, the English cousin to their children, with a strong English accent, which they thought quite amusing.

After that, I worked my way north to Montreal, then on to Ottowa, then to Toronto. I went west to Vancouver, again by train, down the West Coast of America, then crossed by sea from San Fransisco to Yokohama, via Hawaii. I went around Japan. My father had managed to get me a visa for China, which was very much under Mao. I went to Peking, then to the Great Wall, and then down to Shanghai.

I happened to meet a friend in Peking who was working for Alfred Holt, a big shipping line. He and I went to the Great Wall together. I had no connections, whereas he was visiting the Chinese shipping agents who Alfred Holt dealt with.

From there I went to Hong Kong, and on to Singapore. I travelled to Bali, which was wonderful. It was the one stop which was not to do with business. There was one rather simple hotel. We did a lot with the wool trade as a firm, and my father was very friendly with a Dutchman, who was one of our clients. And he had said, "When Peter goes to Indonesia, he must go to Bali." He told me also whom to get hold of, and they took me around to all the dances. There were virtually no foreigners. This

THE STORY OF A FAMILY TRADING COMPANY

Peter Augustus Brandt.

particular Indonesian arranged for me to go to one of the places where they taught the dancing and the music. It was magical. I was so pleased I did that, because when I went later with Liza, it had become a place of great, modern hotels.

I went back to Singapore, then went up through Burma, making a detour to visit Angkor Wat on the way. I had been away a long time by then and was beginning to be keen to get home. I arrived in Calcutta, went to the hotel where I had been booked, and was saluted in the most delightful way by the most marvellous doorman with a terrific cockade on his head and fabulous clothes. "Salam Sahib!" It was such a brilliant welcome that I was no longer in a hurry to go home after that – I had got it out of my system.

I went around India. I went to Ceylon – down one side of India then up the other, travelling mainly by train on a good railway system. I visited Delhi. Then I crossed the border into Pakistan. It was quite concerning. There were soldiers on either side and it was all rather confrontational. I went to Lahore – a beautiful town – then from there to Karachi.

111

I flew to Aden and across the Red Sea. I wanted to go to Eritrea. We did business in Ethiopia, so I went and saw the manager of our client in Addis Ababa. Then I went down to the Red Sea by car, spent a little bit of time there, continued down to Kenya and worked my way south, by air most of the time. I went to the north of Northern Rhodesia and by train overnight to Victoria Falls. Then I made my way into Southern Rhodesia. I had heard that a friend of mine, Michael de Lotbinière, was there. He was a tobacco planter. I rang him up; it was approaching Christmas – the second one I had been away for. I asked him whether he was doing anything particular to celebrate, and he wasn't. He got some sort of turkey and I got a Christmas pudding and I drove out to him. He was living in a round house, one part of which he let me stay in, the other he stayed in. We had Christmas together.

Then I went down into South Africa, where I had some clients. In Cape Town I boarded the SS *Athlone Castle* and came home. My father met me in Southampton. I had been away for two years. He said, "You saw much more than I saw, because you could fly. When I went around in the 20s, I couldn't."

All through my travels, I wrote formal reports to my father at the firm: whom I saw, what they did and any comments they had, what the country was like economically and politically. Then I wrote what I regarded as the tourist bit to my mother.

I had a mini-fling with a Japanese girl, and she asked me if I could get some Chinese silk from Hong Kong. I got it and sent it to her. She was delighted and got me a Kimono, wrapped it up and sent it to England. When that arrived from Japan, my parents wondered whether there was going to be a Japanese daughter-in-law – which, given recent events, was not what they wanted. But they need not have feared.

Rubber

Back at the firm, I became a partner in 1962. But before that, in 1959, I was given the job of looking after our rubber trading company, Pargola, which was in a muddle. It had been run by someone very good. He had retired, leaving two successors who were not nearly so effective. My father was the chairman of the rubber trading company and he had no confidence in the new management, so he had to check practically every contract they took on, which was a useless way of running things, because they spent half their time waiting outside his office to ask whether or not they could buy a hundred tons of rubber for delivery next September, by which time the market had moved, so the deal was pointless. The other partners were saying, "For Heaven's sake, what are you going to do about that company?" He kept saying, "It'll be all right, Peter will do it when he comes back." So that was my first real job and it resulted in a complete reorganisation of the management and a certain amount of pain, because the people at the top had to go.

There was a younger man in the company, John Saxby, whose father had been a senior figure in the rubber trade for many years, and when I was put in, I naturally related immediately to him, because he was my sort of age. I saw what was going on, learned a bit about how the whole thing worked, then talked to him. He told me everything that had to be done. He told me the important things in the business which we had completely neglected. A rubber trading organisation is actually a dealing operation, because a rubber dealer provides the link between the buyer of physical rubber, like Dunlop, and the rubber estate, which is the producer. When the price is high, the rubber buyer will buy as little as he can, because he does not want to have to pay high prices for too long. The rubber estate, conversely, wants to sell as much of its production as it possibly can, at the high prices, and you can therefore deal as far ahead as two years, which means buying or selling for delivery at some point in the future. A rubber dealer resolves that conflict of interest.

This involves the Rubber Exchange. But what we had neglected was the physical side of rubber. You cover your positions by taking out paper contracts, which is a contract to deliver so many tons of a certain kind of rubber, on a particular date. That remains a piece of paper until it

113

eventually matures, and someone ships you ten tons of rubber on that date. But actually, you undo the contract long before that happens, or you convert it to a physical, and you deliver it to Dunlop – but you have fixed the price, and that is the point. That is what a rubber dealer does. But what we had done was become increasingly involved in the paper transactions alone and we were getting it wrong all the time, because we did not actually know what was happening on the physical side. You have to have a large physical business, but one that is actually buying rubber from Singapore and Malaya and having, as your customers, all the major rubber buyers, like Dunlop. If you do not do that, you do not actually know what is happening in the market.

I reorganised things. But it meant I had to make some people redundant, which was quite grim – I was 30-something, with men who were 55. I was as gentle and nice about it as I could be, but they actually had to leave. We did give them some financial security and were as helpful as we possibly could be, but it was not very pleasant. I also knew it was an issue that I could not duck. I had to think the thing out carefully, and think about how I was going to present it to them. Later events proved it was the correct thing to do.

As for the dealing work itself, it was quite tiring, standing up all day on the Exchange floor. But it was very interesting because you talked to the people who had been in the rubber trade all their lives. It was continual trading there, not rings: with some commodities – metal for example – they call the prices at certain times of the day, and the rest of the time the place is empty. Rubber was continuous trade from something like ten in the morning until three or four in the afternoon, and there were contracts being made all over the room, all the time. It was a very big room in Plantation House, very high ceilings, and there would be 50 to 100 people at any given time. But they did not make a lot of noise. It was not at all like these pictures you see of commodity futures, with everybody shouting.

The people I met there were quite different from those I met when I went to visit merchant banks. They were tougher people – commodity dealers. But they were polite and friendly, and told me all that I needed to know. It was the first major responsibility I had, and having learned about it, and having put the reorganisation through, it was then particularly rewarding to see the company actually turn round and make profits. It became a time of expansion.

There was a growing body of Chinese rubber producers who, having gone out to Malaya as 'coolies', had successfully dealt in rubber as a sideline and then gone on to buy formerly European-owned plantations, Up until then William Brandt's hadn't traded with them. John Saxby went out to Malaya and established trading relations with the leading suppliers.

After Rubber

The rubber went quite well for a while, but then conditions in the market became extremely competitive. Rubber dealers depend on price movements to make money, and the price became very static. We therefore had to take quite large risks for very small returns and eventually we concluded it was not worthwhile. But we still had staff – what they now call a 'back office', which was well-organised for shipping goods around the world. I converted that into an export finance company, where we would go to British exporters and say, "Convert your export to India into a sale into a UK fund and we will handle the whole thing. You just deliver the goods to us. We will do the documentation and pay you cash at the time of shipment." We turned that into quite a good business. We also gave credit to overseas buyers of British goods. I did that quite vigorously for about three years.

Working in the partners' room by that time, and in the beginning very much the new boy in the class, I kept quite quiet. But I was thwarted by the conservatism and the difficulty in making any kind of real advances into new ideas. I had to produce enormous arguments and reasons, and prove that it was not risky at all, otherwise they simply would not do it. It was very frustrating.

They were cautious – but they were also rash. They would occasionally do things which were larger than they should have done for the size of the bank, and got into difficulties. At other times they were overly prudent.

One of the problems of a family firm is that people go into it when it might not be right for them. Some of the partners should perhaps not have been bankers. My father was quite vigorous. It was the others who were too cautious. And you had to get consensus all the time, because it was partly their money. So we often ended up with compromises. If one person was against something, you simply could not do it. You had to lobby some of the other partners and explain it to them, and then they would vote for you and persuade the reluctant party.

But they tended to be nervous about doing anything new which they did not really understand. They would say, "We've never done that before." That was their reason for not doing it.

Barings, Rothschilds, Kleinworts

Each bank's character depended very much on the style of the family. Barings were slightly older than we were, rather more worldly, and cleverer. They had a much wider business. We never did capital issues, which the other merchant banks tended to do, which is the thing we had to catch up on later. Barings, Rothschilds and Kleinworts all issued bonds for people, or stocks and shares, but we did not. That was how the merchant banks grew away from trade finance during the 1950s and '60s.

Kleinworts were larger too. They did a lot of trade finance and they did it all over the world. They were run by two brothers, Ernest and Cyril, and were quite imaginative. I remember them both; I got to know Cyril better than Ernest. Then there was Kenneth, Ernest's son. Cyril I always knew as someone who was personally enormously involved in the various activities of the bank. If they had things which were going wrong, he used to say to the various members of the staff, "I worry about your project," so they knew he was thinking about it. Ernest used to cycle to work. They merged with Robert Benson and Lonsdale, which was a great move.

We had nothing much to do with Hambros, but with Schroders we did a certain amount. We shared quite a lot of credits and used to do a lot of German business with them. Again, they were larger than we were.

Tonquist and Argentine Developments

Later, I became the London director of a British-Argentine owned meat company in Smithfield called the Sansinena Company. It was a business that William Brandt's had got into in 1890 at the time of the Baring crisis. The Barings were the main financiers in Argentina at the time, but because of their illiquidity, which had been caused by Argentine bonds, they were not able to continue. There was a big merchant banking group in Argentina called Ernesto Tonquist, who controlled a number of businesses and needed to provide financing facilities for them. One of them was the Sansinena Company, and the story goes that Ernesto Tonquist himself appeared in London in 1890, came to see my great-grandfather Augustus Ferdinand and said, "Because of the Baring crisis, I cannot negotiate Baring bills. Could you give me a line of credit?" Augustus Ferdinand asked, "How much do you need?" Tonquist replied, "I need £750,000," a lot of money in 1890. "Give me a few minutes, I must go and talk to my brothers," replied Augustus Ferdinand, because it was a partnership between him, Alfred Ernst and Arthur Henry. They said yes. They gave him a line of three-quarters of a million and we then started, as a firm, financing exports of Argentine meat, and quite a lot of other things: Argentine grain, Argentine sugar. We continued doing a great deal of that until we sold the bank in 1972. When Sansinena established a company in London in the 1920s, Great-Uncle Henry became one of the founding directors. His son then took over and I succeeded him in 1970.

National and Grindlays take a two-thirds interest

National and Grindlays got involved in William Brandt's because we were short of capital, having had three major losses. The first was related to a timber operation in the Cameroons, where the timber agency business represented a timber shipper and sold his production, probably in Europe, not just in the United Kingdom. I do not know all the details, but I think they had lent him quite a lot of money in order to exploit the timber reserves, and he went bust, so he never shipped the timber. The money was lost. Then there was a wool dealer who went bankrupt, and we had larger amounts out to him than we should have done.

Then, most importantly, there was the famous salad oil swindle, which was in 1964 or '65. There was a man in New York called Tino de Angelis who carried out an enormous swindle in vegetable oils. Books were written about it. He conned a large number of New York banks, trading houses and commodity firms. We had lent more money than we should have to one supposedly perfectly reputable New York investment house, who were deeply involved, and they went bankrupt because of the swindle. If we had actually made enquiries, we would have found that the management of that particular investment bank had changed dramatically, almost between the date of the information we had obtained, which said they were a well-respected house, and the time that we actually lent the money. And we should have been alerted to the fact that they were paying slightly over the market, which, if they were as good as they were made out to be, they should not have had to do. That should always be a danger sign.

If there had been just one or two disasters, it would have been all right. But there were three in a row. The partners became terribly demoralised and could not see what to do. They were for selling out and almost chucked their hand in. My father less so, but the other two were very dispirited. I stood out and said, "You cannot do that. Let's get Cooper Brothers to give us some advice." Cooper Brothers were not actually very helpful. They put in a man called Obrien Newman, who was really a fixer. We wanted someone with greater expertise.

But the long and short of it was that National and Grindlays Bank got involved. They were what was called an 'Eastern Exchange Bank' in those days: a London registered bank, but with most of its business in India and East Africa, where they had branches. They were the fourth largest bank in India. They were interested in getting into London on a bigger scale and developing merchant banking.

National and Grindlays came in in 1965 and took two-thirds of the capital by way of addition, by taking up new shares, adding something in the order of two or three million pounds to the capital. The Brandt family were left with a third.

I was not involved in the negotiations. A man called Henry Benson, who was a senior partner at Cooper Brothers, was very involved.

And the Bank of England helped – at least at first. Lord Aldington was the chairman of National and Grindlays. He was about 55 and keen to do things. We did not have a lot of capital and they had two-thirds, so he was put on the Board, and his chief general manager, Douglas Caley, was also put on it and provided a lot of support – a very good man indeed who had run exchange control for the Indian Government during the War. The business expanded enormously thanks to Aldington's encouragement; we came up with proposals and developed new areas of business and expertise and we all had a lot of fun.

It was very positive indeed. Within a year, he had appointed me as managing director, which caused frightful upset within the family, because they were all jealous and they were going to jolly well try and see that I did not actually do anything at all. It was quite unpleasant. But Aldington supported me very hard and we won through after a battle.

They tried to pretend that the fact that National and Grindlays had come in with a two-thirds interest was not going to make any difference at all, which was naïve. By that time, we had quite a number of young men who, like me, were all raring to do something different and new. It was quite clear that the younger generation in William Brandt's wanted to advance and progress, and they saw the arrival of Grindlays as an opportunity to do that. Aldington backed us to the hilt and was extremely good at saying things like, "Well, just because we haven't done it before, there's no reason not to look at it," which was the exact opposite to the way the older partners had been operating. He made the partners look at things and if he said, "Yes, I think we ought to do that," they could not really say no. So we made gradual progress. But it was frustrating nevertheless. There was a lot of nervous strain over the whole thing.

Sometimes I considered leaving, because it was bringing me into so much conflict with my family, but I never made any moves to do so and I knew I never would. There was resistance for the sake of resistance. I would wake up in the middle of the night, think about it, get angry, think it over again, all between two, three and four o'clock in the morning.

Liza knew what was happening and she was as supportive as she could be, but she could not actually change the attitudes of the old men. It was Aldington who did that. It all seemed to go on for a long time, but actually we were probably over it within two or three years.

Under Grindlays we went into shipping finance, and particularly Greek ship-owners. We already had experience with export finance, for example Spain. Spain was classified as a B country, so people were inherently slightly nervous of it, but we actually knew that it was a perfectly good risk.

'A' countries were obviously the United States, West Germany, France, where credit is very easy to come by and things were extremely competitive, so the margins were not very good. But in Spain, you got very attractive margins. Then Spain gradually developed and business became more competitive, so we looked elsewhere for up-and-coming B class countries. Greece was one of them. Instead of actually doing export finance from the United Kingdom to Greece, we started doing shipping finance for the Greeks, which then developed.

It was very successful. There was a shipping boom at that time, 1966, for almost ten years. There were two other people who principally developed that business. We would go to Athens from time to time and meet them.

In practical terms, my appointment as chief executive meant I was responsible for the general management of William Brandt's, in all its aspects. The particular department I looked after directly was Foreign Exchange and Money Market. They were originally divided into different departments and I amalgamated them, because there was a huge interchange between them. That too was very successful.

We became very active in ordinary banking in Eurodollar deposits. All our Greek ship-owner finance, for instance, was done in dollars. We took in dollar deposits and lent out dollars. We developed that also in South America during the same period and did quite a lot of business in Mexico, and a certain amount in Argentina – again, using Eurodollar deposits. We were short-term Eurodollar lenders.

We did not necessarily see a great many people in the Eurodollar world. The other merchant banks were also quite important players in it, but we all had our own areas of speciality. I think Hill Samuel did quite a lot of Greek ship-owner business. Otherwise it was big American banks and some of the British ones. In South America, Barings and Rothschilds were big competitors, especially in Mexico, and especially Rothschilds. We competed for customers. There was not any poaching. If they were poaching our customers, we were poaching theirs.

I knew Evelyn de Rothschild because we had been at Cambridge together. He was slightly aloof, perhaps, but not in a derogatory sense. He kept to himself and had his own friends. We were in the same lodging house, but I did not see a great deal of him. Later I used to see some of the Rothschild's executives and we were always quite friendly. They knew we were competing for the same people. They would go to the Mexican Ministry of Finance; I would go the next morning. We had an agent in Mexico and he developed business for us which did not really compete, or did not appear to compete, with Rothschilds. Rothschilds were dealing more with the Government. We tended to deal more with private enterprises. There are some large firms there; we financed quite a lot of the steel industry. We financed a fishing fleet; our principal finance was actually the supply of Rolls Royce diesel engines for fishing boats. Those were two big deals we did, but otherwise it was a lot of largish, privately owned companies whom we financed.

We had some very good Mexican friends. We financed one Mexican ship-owner, who was quite successful. He became a good friend, but I lost touch with him after I stopped banking.

If I went on a long trip abroad – which was usually half PR exercise, half developing business – I would take Liza. I took her to Mexico and I took her to Argentina. Not that I think it made a huge amount of difference to business to have her with me. It was good at main receptions. Lord Aldington always took the view that if you were working hard, it was nice to be able to relax with your wife in the evenings. It made the thing less intense. The children were not yet away at boarding school, but we had an au pair who looked after them and my mother was always extremely good and would have them at weekends.

We also developed insurance broking around that time and took a one-third interest in one of the leading firms in Lloyds, which produced a great deal of deposit and banking business. It was called Sturge. One of the Sturges wanted to sell out and we helped the new generation, David Coleridge, to move up in the management and begin to manage Sturge. William Brandt's had been one of the early broking members of Lloyds.

One of the attractions of shipping finance was that you got a massive flow of freights over the accounts all the time. You would have a ship out on charter, and every month, a substantial sum of money would come in and be distributed – crew payments, stores, harbour dues, all sorts of things – and then amortisation of the loan. Then, at the beginning of the next month, there would be another great mass. It was very attractive.

Of course, you did not pay all the bills in dollars, you paid them in Deutschmarks, or wherever the currency was in which the accounts had arisen. We exchanged that within the bank and made a commission on it.

My relationship with my father gradually improved. It had been quite difficult for him and the partners to see exactly what they were

William Edward Brandt. Portrait by Norman Hepple, R.A. 1963

supposed to be doing after National and Grindlays came in. From one day to the next, they were no longer running things. But a role gradually developed for them. Less so for cousin Willy, who gradually retired. My father became Chairman about 1969 or '70. He was there every day and chaired all the committee meetings. He had, of course, a huge range of contacts, particularly in Germany, and also in the City. It was PR as well as chairing. His advice was useful. The other area that we expanded into at the same time was property finance, which we had not touched upon until then. And the end of the 1960s was quite a favourable time for doing it. It went well.

As short-term bankers with our roots in trade finance, we had never been involved with the capital requirements of industry, so we developed a business in which we leased capital equipment. That too was successful. Sometimes we leased a ship, but mainly it was capital equipment. That was another area which expanded quite satisfactorily. We had everything departmentalised, so we knew how each department was doing at the end of each month. All the banking departments were the ones which gained immediately from the flow of this new business over the banking. The other departments which were set up as profit centres, took longer to develop. But the bank benefitted straight away, which is the advantage.

That was a result of Grindlays' support and encouragement and their strength, because they were bigger than us. They had a big deposit base, so we could always get all the money we wanted for these various areas of expansion. Grindlays used to participate directly in some of the things we did. We would build a consortium if something was very large. We took a share and ran the consortium. Grindlays and other banks whom we approached would participate. So it was of value to Grindlays because it was feeding them with direct business as well as their gain through William Brandt's.

Grindlays were at 23 Fenchurch Street, and we were still at number 36. It was a very short walk. We would spend quite a lot of time visiting Grindlays and they would spend a lot of time visiting us. We had credit committees at least once a week and a Grindlays man would always attend. Douglas Caley came to start with.

The Sale of Brandt's

Things went extremely successfully from 1966 to 1970 or '71. The shareholders of National and Grindlays were Lloyds Bank at 25%, and the public. Lord Aldington wanted to get the American Citibank involved, because he knew, with National and Grindlays as the fourth largest bank in India, and a great deal of aid passing from the United States to that country, that if he had a big and powerful American link, he could handle a lot of that aid. He succeeded in persuading Citibank to take a share of National and Grindlays. The share structure he devised was quite complicated.

At the same time, Douglas Caley retired and another man from Grindlays became the chief general manager, John Gordon. He was a much less powerful character than Douglas Caley. And I think that

Aldington, looking across the waters at Citibank, wanted to copy its structure. There was this man called Walter Wriston who was a big figure on the international banking scene. He was chairman and chief executive of Citibank. I think Aldington rather fancied doing the same thing himself.

Aldington got in some consultants, McKinseys, and said, "I have to reorganise the whole of this Group." They did exactly what they were told and wrote a report in which they said that Lord Aldington should be the chairman and chief executive rolled into one. He had always lectured us, as young men, that the roles of chairman and chief executive should be kept apart. But when it came to himself, he decided otherwise. He became chief executive, but he was not really a very good one. He was a very good non-executive chairman, because he gave everybody a lot of support – he gingered everybody along and asked the right questions, and everybody got on with it. The moment he became chief executive, his role and attitude changed completely. He started telling us what to do, and, being a politician, he created an enormous amount of politics inside the Group, which was a great shame, because hitherto, we had simply got on with our work.

Instead of running their share of William Brandt's by having two people on the Board and keeping an eye on what we were doing and attending the credit committees, Grindlays now produced a mass of rules and regulations setting out the basis on which we should operate. Of course, as soon as you do that, people begin to find ways to circumvent the rules. It is not a very sensible way of doing things unless you are a huge group, and it was not necessary in the case of William Brandt's, which had a staff of 300. Nor was it necessary to act as if something was going wrong. Nothing was. The bank was proceeding perfectly satisfactorily. Part of the McKinsey Report also recommended that the whole Group, i.e. National and Grindlays and William Brandt's, should be divided into divisions, so there would be an overseas banking division, which actually was primarily India. That was all well-established and easy. They got a chap who was in charge of the overseas banking division and he ran the branches of National and Grindlays in India and East Africa. Then there was a finance division and a merchant banking division. There may have been other divisions as well. We were to be part of the merchant banking division. But the one thing that McKinseys were never able to solve was, how do you have a merchant banking division as part of Grindlays, and a merchant bank which ran quite independently? We argued about this for a long time. McKinseys never came up with a proper solution.

We said that to try and make a merchant bank like William Brandt's a part of a large commercial bank simply would not work. The philosophies are quite different. Commercial bankers have a quite different view of banking from merchant bankers. Merchant bankers tend to take dealing risks, which is part of their whole approach. Occasionally you stick your neck out and sometimes it goes right, sometimes it goes wrong. Commercial bankers with large boards find it extremely difficult to explain things when they have gone wrong, therefore they do not have quite the same entrepreneurial approach, so the type of people they employ are quite different. Oil and water do not mix. We kept on saying this. "You will lose the people in William Brandt's, because they will be deadened by the Grindlay bankers." Nothing wrong with the Grindlay bankers – they were extremely good at doing their job, but what they could not do was grasp what we were about. We had a long, almost two-year argument about it. In the end, Aldington said, "Well, we're not going to resolve this." By that time there was a lot of unease and unpleasantness, certainly in William Brandt's.

I became unhappy. It was not possible to operate. I saw the whole thing, the whole life of William Brandt's, its whole long history entwined with our family, just eventually going down the drain. What Aldington then said was, "The best thing for me to do is to buy you out." We certainly did not want that to happen. We would have liked to have found someone who could have taken over National and Grindlays' share, but Aldington refused that, despite there being people who were interested.

The Bank of England got quite involved in the discussions, because the Bank of England had actually written into the original purchase agreement that they would have the ultimate say, and they had hinted, quite strongly, that they would be prepared to encourage someone else to buy us. We had someone else to buy us, but at the last moment, O'Brien, who was the Bank of England's Governor, backed away. He did not want a confrontation with Aldington. Aldington, at that time, was politically very powerful because Edward Heath had just been re-elected in 1970, and Heath depended very much on him for advice. He had a house down in Kent and Aldington lived down there too, not far from Rye. Aldington and I had a very good relationship until the end, when we were in dispute, and I would often go and see him at six in the evening, in his office. We would chat about this and that, then he would say, "Oh, Lord! Got to go and see Ted tomorrow." Or, "Ted wants to come and see me," and Heath would talk over his problems with him. Therefore, I always assumed, O'Brien's peerage was a consideration. He wanted to be on the right side of Edward Heath, and he thought that if he fought with Aldington, he would not be. I suspect that is what happened.

In any case, O'Brien backed away. He had previously told us that he had it in his gift and would assist us. Then quite suddenly he did not. We felt very betrayed. He actually let us down very badly. He and the Deputy Governor acted like civil servants and simply covered themselves.

By then the row had become quite nasty, and it was actually uncomfortable to go in and work, because I always knew there was going to be something cropping up. So, in the end, we agreed to sell and we actually negotiated a very good deal for the family. But when it was all over, we sat there, and there was 160 years of history down the pan. My father and I were very upset about it. I may have suggested that my relations with him were not always especially warm, but right at the end, they were the best that they had ever been, because he and I felt the same way about the firm.

In retrospect, one wonders: would there have been a possibility, if we had not brought National and Grindlays in, of the bank surviving?

It would have been quite difficult; I do not know whether we had the expertise to make it survive. We would have had to have specialised and become experts – what they now call "niche players": you develop an expertise for which you do not require a great deal of capital. We did not have that kind of background, and we were in a business which was becoming more and more competitive, and therefore less and less profitable, and we needed the capital to move out of it into other areas.

Once we had realised we were going to have to sell out to Grindlays, it all happened quite quickly, at least in today's terms. It seemed to take a terribly long time as we were going on, partly because Aldington had to check with Citibank the whole time. It was several months. A lot of quite senior people left. I warned Aldington that they would, but he disregarded that advice. He was very annoyed of course. But he had been told.

Very quickly I went from being somebody deeply involved in the City, with quite a lot of say, to having no role whatsoever. I did ask myself, "Well, shall I retire?" But I was only 40 and it would have been ridiculous to retire then. Financially I could have, but I think I would have been very bored and I do not think it would have been right to. I did stay in the City for about five years, but it was not successful. We were trying to repeat the past and you cannot do that. My father also stayed in the City – he came with us, so to speak.

When we sold out, they changed the bank's name and called it Brandts Limited instead of William Brandt's, Sons and Company. My successor took over in about July 1972. Our balance sheet at that time was around 200 million pounds – not very big in today's terms, but quite large. We were about the fifth or sixth largest merchant bank. Within two or three years, he had doubled the balance sheet to 400 million. But most of that was speculative property and in 1974 or '76, when the property market crashed, they had enormous bad debts and the bank was absorbed into Grindlays and became one of their departments. It ceased to be a member of the Accepting Houses Committee and my successor left. That really was the end of the whole thing. I was sorry it had happened. But in a way, one said, "Serves them right."

Peter Augustus Brandt, photograph taken by *The Times* in 1972 after the final sale of the bank.

Technically, we could have refused to sell out to Grindlays. We could not be forced, but it would have been very stupid to have stayed on. They could have done other things: they could have said, "Right, we're going to run it our way, and you can all leave." They could have fired us. They had control.

My overriding sorrow was that we were not there in William Brandt's any more, and shortly afterwards, William Brandt's did not exist. But then one had to go on with one's life.

After Brandt's

We were left with nothing except some finance. We had no involvements, except that I was a director of the London Life Association and had been since 1962. And in 1970 I had become a director of Sansinena and I continued to do that. That gave me links in the City. The new regime at William Brandt's were not very keen on doing Argentine meat finance, because they did not understand Argentina. Martin Mays-Smith left William Brandt's and went to Kleinworts, after which

Kleinworts did the banking for Sansinena, until there was not really any serious banking to do.

With a group of people from William Brandt's I joined a firm called Edward Bates, which, with the secondary banking crisis, got into difficulties. It was not a good time to be starting things up. It was a small merchant bank. The people were entirely different. They were doing a different sort of business. There was a boom through 1968–72, and they bought and sold stakes in companies. They took a stake in property and they were making a lot of money. Fairly second-class business, and quite speculative. They were not dealing with first-class firms. They were dealing with entrepreneurs who would buy a field and get planning permission on it – that kind of thing.

For about five years I was there doing much the same thing as I had been doing at William Brandt's. We were developing a foreign exchange department, money market, and a certain amount of banking. But my heart was not in it as it had been at William Brandt's. Then it began to get difficult.

The principal player was a man called Jimmy Gammell, who was a Scotsman and the senior partner of Ivory & Sime in Edinburgh. He did not pay very good attention to it. He allowed people to do what they liked. There was not any proper control and no real co-ordination. It was a mistake to have gone there. If I had consulted Liza properly about it, she would have met the people involved and I am sure she would have said, "You should steer clear of that." But I did not, much to my regret. In about 1977 it was taken over and became the Allied Arab Bank.

My father joined us at Bates for a bit, then left, retired, and looked after his picture collection. He died in 1978, so there was not much of his life left. He had begun to have strokes. He had never been terribly fit throughout his life.

I think he was quite sorrowful at the end, because of what had happened. Like me, he did not talk about it very much, believing that one should never tell a story and moan. You have to accept what happens in life and move on to the next thing, not complain about the past.

After the City

A man called Felix Atkins lived across the road from us in Suffolk. We went there from London, mainly at weekends, and he would come and have a drink and talk about his company Atkins Fulford, in which he was a 50% shareholder. They had done quite interesting work with the big coal-fired power stations.

Around the time I left the City, he decided to go and live on the Isle of Man. I tried to persuade him not to, but he was determined. I asked what he was going to do about the business and he said, "Oh well, we're going to sell it." As a sort of afterthought, he said, "You know about these things, perhaps you could help us sell up?" He gave me the balance sheet. It was a good little balance, a good little company – not large, but very profitable and liquid, and I said, "If you want to sell it, I might be interested." I got a friend, who was an industrial consultant, to have a look and see if there was anything I would not be able to understand. He gave it a clean bill of health. Atkins said to me, "Well, if you're going to come in as a shareholder, I'll leave my money in after all." So I bought out Arthur Fulford, which was a very good way of going in, because I bought 50% rather than 100%, and I kept Fulford on the Board to give me advice, so that we had a carry-over from the past. He was extremely helpful and it was great fun.

It subsequently developed very satisfactorily throughout the seventies. Atkins died in 1979 and about a year later I bought his share, so in about 1980 I became the 100% shareholder. It was very small. It had a managing director – who actually did everything – an accounts clerk, and a secretary. Then a workforce. I got in new management underneath him. He was not very good at delegating, so that required quite a lot of attention. Then he retired, and the man I got in as works director became the managing director. The business diversified away from power station work and became involved with water filtration.

I used to spend Mondays and Fridays there at first, then less time as things went on, having developed a management and financial control system which I operated myself. I really enjoyed it.

I thought I would miss the City, but I did not really. I could never have gone back, because it changed dramatically in its whole style. The merchant banks no longer do the same business as we did then; it is all different. I also suspect that the people are all very much cleverer. I was talking to Peter Spira once. Peter Spira was himself very bright: he was a scholar at school, he may have been a scholar at Cambridge, and he said to me, "You would be astonished at the high qualifications and intelligence of the people we are taking in. You and I would not get a look in nowadays."

I used to help Bill McAlpine with his railway interests. Bill McAlpine owned the Flying Scotsman locomotive and some coaches. He started it as a hobby and it became a business. He had quite substantial assets which had to be employed for this and they were not being looked after properly, in the sense that there were no financial controls and no real figures. There was a balance sheet at the end of the year. He asked me to become his deputy, looking after that, so I did.

I was a main board member of the National Rivers Authority, which was the regulatory side of water privatisation and also a regional board member for the Anglian Region. There were ten regions in the NRA and each had a local chairman. That work I also found very absorbing.

I continued coaching for Trinity College Boat Club at Cambridge for 35 years, until 1998, at which point I felt the time had come to stop.

I had also been involved for many years as a trustee of Gainsborough's House, the birthplace of the painter, Thomas Gainsborough, a local museum in Sudbury, Suffolk, dedicated to his life and works.

Summing Up

Looking back, I am pleased with my achievements as chief executive of William Brandt's. I enjoyed being a member of the National Rivers Authority, and one of the most rewarding things about that was doing something for my country and for the environment. To have done that towards the end of my working life was a source of great pleasure and satisfaction. I am very grateful for my ongoing relationship with the

Trinity College Boat Club at Cambridge. I enjoyed meeting new generations of undergraduates, spending time with them and helping them in what they were doing.

What I most regret is the loss of William Brandt's. But, as I said, you must not look back. You should always look forward.

Epilogue

In viewing the family through the lens of the bank, I am very aware that not all family members were directly involved, and indeed that sadly the bank no longer exists. However, as a family we share a common heritage, and my objective in publishing this book has been to make this record available to the wider family and to the general public. Perhaps it may help to re-establish connections, remember stories and foster appreciation of the wide ranging and creative talents and work involvements across the generations, both past and present. My greatest wish is that distant cousins may share an interest in the history of their forebears.

MAPS

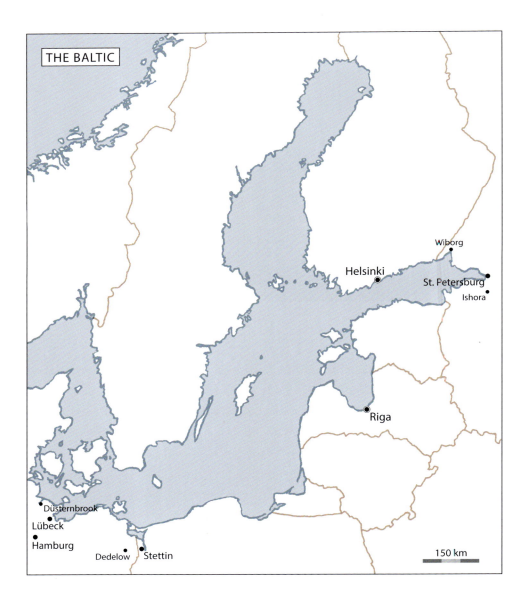